HOW TO BEAT THE PRO FOOTBALL POINTSPREAD

HOW TO BEAT THE PRO FOOTBALL POINTSPREAD

A COMPREHENSIVE, NO-NONSENSE
GUIDE TO PICKING NFL WINNERS

BOBBY SMITH

SKYHORSE PUBLISHING

Skyhorse Publishing books may be purchased in bulk at special discounts for sales promotion, corporate gifts, fund-raising, or educational purposes. Special editions can also be created to specifications. For details, contact the Special Sales Department, Skyhorse Publishing, 555 Eighth Avenue, Suite 903, New York, NY 10018 or info@skyhorsepublishing.com.

www.skyhorsepublishing.com

10 9 8 7 6 5 4 3 2 1

Library of Congress Cataloging-in-Publication Data

Smith, Robert James, 1957-
How to beat the pro football pointspread : a comprehensive, no-nonsense guide to picking NFL winners / Bobby Smith.
p. cm.

Includes Index.

ISBN-13: 978-1-60239-307-3 (alk. paper)
ISBN-10: 1-60239-307-9 (alk. paper)
1. Football—Betting—United States. 2. Sports betting—United States. 3. National Football League. I. Title.
GV954.3.S65 2008
796.332—dc22
2008025267

Printed in the United States of America

To my beloved Theresa, sweetest home favorite since '03

Table of Contents

Preface

There are two possible outcomes. If the result confirms the hypothesis, then you've made a measurement. If the result is contrary to the hypothesis, then you've made a discovery.
—*Enrico Fermi*, Italian physicist

A **GUY CALLS UP** his bookie.

"Hey Louie, how you doing, it's Bill. Listen, how did I do on the baseball today?"

Louie: "On baseball, you lost a grand."

Bill: "What? A thousand? Oh no. God, that's terrible! Well, how did I do on the football then?"

Louie: "On football, you lost a grand."

Bill: "Another thousand?! You mean I lost two thousand today? I don't understand it, this is unbelievable ... Tell me how I did on the basketball?"

Louie: "On the basketball, you lost a grand."

Bill: "Three thousand dollars? It just can't be ... what am I going to tell my wife? This is just terrible!"

Louie: "So listen, Joe, you wanna put something on the hockey game tonight?"

Bill: "Hockey? What do I know about hockey?"

The guts of this well-worn joke, of course, is that the typical bettor is a pathological loser who is deluded into thinking that simply generating an opinion makes him supremely qualified to wager and to win. He doesn't follow hockey, and his lack of knowledge of it is matched by his understanding of the three sports he knows. He has the losses to prove it. The background premise that might fly by unnoticed is that the bookmaker, upon gaining $3,000 from the bettor in one afternoon, still has an insatiable hunger for more, and no regard for the well-being of the bettor.

According to figures reported by gaming correspondent Stephen Nover, football bettors have lost their way. "Thanks to a strong football season," wrote Nover on February 15, 2007, "Nevada sports books won $191 million this past year. That's a 51 percent increase from 2005." Clearly, there is an urgent need for a resource that challenges and improves upon the current state of affairs and teaches football bettors how to win. So, here we are.

The National Football League's goals and NFL bettor's goals are mutually exclusive. The NFL operates in what I like to call "Straight-Up America," where most people root for fun and self-esteem. Pointspreads do not exist. Pointspread players can live in Straight-Up America, but the smarter ones eventually move to ATS World, where they absorb more pertinent information—the information that's critical to their winning on Sunday. "ATS" is a common abbreviation for "Against the Spread." Straight-Up is often referred to as simply "SU." The two short references will be used throughout the book.

The book sheds light on the ranges of NFL results that usually occur year after year, yet still seem to puzzle many people. Remember, cavemen couldn't predict weather unless they saw it coming at them. Today, we have a pretty good idea of what the weather will be at any particular spot in the world, a week to ten days before it gets there. It's a similar kind of look-ahead ability that the smart NFL bettor must strengthen if he is to move beyond a misinformed routine of circling hunches on an office pool ticket, or waking up on Sunday morning game-day, scratching the head, and forcing fantasies for the sake of making wagers. The process of picking more NFL winners than before starts with the realization that we will rarely know as much as we think we know and even when we *do*, it's not always easy to retain and recall that knowledge. The chapters herein are grouped into three sections, the first being "The Mindset." The objective of this first section is to gradually draw distinctions between groups of people who melt into the landscape of the NFL audience and make it hard to pin down what it really takes to be right and win money vs. the spread on a consistent basis. It will examine:

- Perceptions of fans who do not wager vs. perceptions of the men (and women) who do, and how the former can set traps for the latter;
- The difference between having an opinion and expecting something to happen because you've seen it happen before;
- Learning to de-emphasize the easily seen and the commonly known, and where to look for critical information that exists but is largely unseen;

- Understanding that math we all learned in junior high school can be employed as confidence-boosting and eye-opening tools in the process of making NFL projections;
- Becoming comfortable with prioritizing coaches, and de-prioritizing players;
- Gradually tuning out the presence of the bookmaker, a mere middleman at best, friend of the devil at worst;
- And knowing when you are being fed a bunch of bull by so-called handicapping experts cutting corners at your expense.

Tuning in minds to what is really going on in the NFL and the wagering marketplace will give every person in the $12 billion universe of NFL bettors a better opportunity to become more sophisticated, selective, and successful. As the book progresses through the next two sections, the intent is to set the reader on a progressive and confidence-building path lined with facts that have remained off the radar for decades. Readers will learn how to minimize popular but damaging traps and position themselves to recognize and capitalize upon more valuable opportunities. New takes on the football wagering practice include instruction on how to anticipate next season's "surprise" and "disappointment" teams before they happen, and learning to think along with the coaches leading up to game day. To help improve the readers' organizational skills and focus within this discipline, specific classes of situations that arise during an NFL season are demonstrated. Important historical data, and specific examples of successes and mistakes are included. For further empowerment, instruction on building and maintaining an effective arsenal of information resources is also discussed.

When the NFL itself, and the concept of wagering on it are each demystified, you can begin to see things that were not previously apparent, gaining the confidence to engage in your own more sophisticated trial-and-error processes to help fine-tune your skills. You learn from mistakes, lose bad habits, and pick up good ones.

As an assistant coach for the Denver Broncos said about the head coach Mike Shanahan, "One of the great things Mike taught me was that sometimes you get some ideas that aren't right. And you have to let them go. It's easy to say as a coach, 'I'm going to make this work. I'm the one who made this decision.' But he always hounded us, 'Hey, if you make a mistake on a player, if you make a mistake in a game, let it go. Go on to the next one. That's part of the job.'"

The NFL wagerer needs to take the same approach. When you win, you made a measurement. When you lose, you made a mistake. Let it go, but only after learning something from it that minimizes future losses and makes for more wins. In that case, you've made a discovery.

HOW TO BEAT THE PRO FOOTBALL POINTSPREAD

Part One
The Mindset

Smarter Than the Average Fan

IT'S A LAZY Labor Day weekend on Long Island and our totally-unconnected-to-the-Mafia Italian side of the family is riding out the last rays of holiday sun at a backyard barbeque. Kids bark. Dogs cry. Relatives yap. The men kick around the work and the sports. Cousin-in-law Eric is a big fan of the New York Jets, a police officer, and a terrific guy. He and more than 70,000 others of his ilk make a pilgrimage to the Meadowlands in East Rutherford, New Jersey, eight times every autumn to revel in the aura they call Gang Green.

Eric's enthusiasm and intensity for the Jets exceeds mine by about four football fields, but I have a handle on that team. A pretty good one, I've been thinking. A position that could be leveraged successfully in about a week for Opening Day of the 2005 season. But maybe there was something eluding me about the guys in the gas station uniforms—egad, the only New York sports team that wears green. Perhaps he could tell me something about the Jets that I didn't already know.

"Yo', Eric. What do you think about the Jets this season?"

"For starters, we're going to kill the Chiefs next Sunday!" Eric's brain has been hard-wired with green insulation, programmed to hold nothing but the highest hopes for the Jets. "We got rid of that idiot offensive coordinator Hackett, the new guy will get more out of the offense, Chad Pennington's arm is better after that surgery, the defense is great, and the Chiefs' defense is terrible!"

Yow. There are 180-degree differences between us in every point he made. But that's what happens when worlds collide. Eric lives in Straight-Up America, where the football followers are regular, rooting NFL fans with an allegiance to a logo. They are vested only on an emotional level. My people—the ones who tackle the tricky tests of investing on the outcome of NFL games—live in another dimension called ATS World.

For our *Sports Reporter* publication—a weekly advance guide for the ATS Man—we've already targeted the Kansas City Chiefs as our Best Bet of the opening NFL weekend. A week later at this very time of the afternoon, the Chiefs, a 3-point favorite—would be hosting Eric's J-E-T-S: Jets, Jets, Jets!

Eric's enthusiasm is based partly on each team's place in the NFL world at the conclusion of the prior season. The Jets finished it with a 10-6 won-loss record, beat San Diego on the road in a wild card playoff game, then lost at Pittsburgh the following weekend in a game they could, and probably should, have won. Had they won it, they would have played in the AFC Championship Game. So for Eric and others like him, the perception of the Jets was a team "one game away from playing for the Super Bowl." After having missed the playoffs the season before that, the needle was pointing up for the Jets as far as he and the rest of the rabid rooters were concerned.

By contrast, the Chiefs had a 7-9 won-loss record the year before, and had allowed 27.2 points—almost 4 touchdowns—per game. Kansas City's average defensive yield—points scored per game by the other team—was two scores greater than the 16.6 points per game allowed by the Jets.

Because Eric is family and only because he's family, he deserves to be warned, spared from what would almost certainly amount to a disappointing day off in front of the television next Sunday afternoon. I, ATS Man, would swoop down and save Straight-Up Man from certain doom in an idealistic gesture of kindness. Diplomatically deferring to the possibility of his Jets having a fine season when all is said and done, I nevertheless caution him to prepare for the worst next Sunday; that it could very well be Kansas City—not the Jets—doing the killing before his very eyes.

"What?! Are you crazy?!"

Kids quit barking. Dogs cease crying. Uncles glare. Aunties stare. They brace for the worst-case scenario—an uncomfortable, alcohol-fueled conflict. They are relieved to hear me respond calmly.

"We're not arguing. I'm telling you there are several key elements to this match-up that you and your people may be overlooking."

NFL home teams, taken as a group, do not have losing seasons. NFL home teams win about six out of every ten games. History—staring back in the face of anyone eyeing Figure 1-1—spells it all out. The percentages vary from season to season, but the 14-year range displayed in the table shows a season-high home-team win rate of 63.6 percent, and a low of 54.1 percent. This is purely Straight-Up wins, with the point-spread not considered. In any given season, 22-33 percent of NFL teams will win at least 75 percent (6) of their regular-season home games. The Chiefs, in fact, were only sixteen games removed from a 2003 season in which they had won all eight regular season games on their home field, the second time in seven seasons they were 8-0 in games played in Arrowhead Stadium.

"It's hard to win on the road in our league. It's hard to win on the road, I don't care where you're going." Sean Payton of the New Orleans Saints said that

NFL Home Teams	W	L	SU Win %	Running SU Win %
1993	131	103	56.0%	56.0%
1994	136	97	58.4%	57.2%
1995	151	99	60.4%	58.3%
1996	157	93	62.8%	59.5%
1997	151	99	60.4%	59.7%
1998	159	91	63.6%	60.3%
1999	155	103	60.1%	60.3%
2000	146	112	56.6%	59.8%
2001	143	115	55.4%	59.3%
2002	156	110	58.6%	59.2%
2003	163	103	61.3%	59.4%
2004	151	115	56.8%	59.2%
2005	155	111	58.3%	59.1%
2006	144	122	54.1%	58.8%
ALL	2,098	1,473	58.8%	58.8%

FIGURE 1-1

on September 16, 2006, just two weeks into his debut season as an NFL head coach, influenced by the Great Masters before him:

10/15/01: Tony Dungy, Indianapolis Colts: "They got 31 points and it's hard to win on the road when you give up 31 points."

11/24/03: Marvin Lewis, Cincinnati Bengals: "It's tough to win on the road anytime in the NFL, no matter where you're playing it at."

10/6/06: Marty Schottenheimer, San Diego Chargers: "Regardless of where you go, it's hard to win on the road in this league."

12/20/06: Romeo Crennell, Cleveland Browns: "It's always tough to win on the road in the NFL."

The coaches all know the deal. So do the players. The Straight-Up Media reports their insider quotes to Straight-Up Fan all the time, but Straight-Up Fan is a little slow on the uptake. The moment this game at Kansas City landed on the Jets' schedule and they were mandated to fly there and play a game, the odds were against them winning it. History—not Jets history, not Chiefs history, but across-the-board, big-picture NFL history—said as much. As if the task wasn't difficult enough, some under-the-radar obstacles were aligning themselves to make it even tougher.

Paul Hackett, the "idiot" referenced by Eric, was replaced as Jets' offensive coordinator by Mike Heimerdinger after the 2004 season. For several seasons,

NY Jets	PF	PA
2004	20.6	16.6
2003	17.7	18.7
2002	22.8	20.3

FIGURE 1-2

Hackett had taken a lot of heat from the Jets fans and the New York media for what these outsiders perceived as an under-performing offense.

The criticism reached a tipping point after the Jets were knocked out of the playoffs in Pittsburgh on January 15, 2005. It was a game the Jets were in position to win despite not scoring an offensive touchdown—a situation not uncommon to good teams in the NFL. For instance, when the Baltimore Ravens won the Super Bowl in 2000, it came on the heels of a five-week run in October and November where they failed to score an offensive touchdown, yet won four of the five games. Overlooking the good things and convinced they knew better than credentialed, specialized professionals, the keyboard quarterbacks and airwave administrators launched into an angry crescendo:

"Paul Hackett needs to be fired. Too conservative, few aggressive plays . . ."
"I hope to hear within forty-eight to seventy-two hours that Paul Hackett is out of a job . . . in the real world, he would have been fired for doing his job so poorly."

On January 19, Hackett resigned, which wasn't good enough for some of the more radical Gang Greeners, and prompted one angry blogger to write the following:

"I was hoping for some public humiliation, perhaps a flogging. Or maybe make Hackett run draw plays by himself in Times Square during rush hour. By resigning, Hackett can be perceived as a sympathetic figure, a man who knew his time was up and bowed out gracefully. [But] This guy was awful and he deserves his time in the spotlight of Hades . . . Jets fans are still twitching at his 5-yard pass plays on third-and-6, and his 2-yard quick outs on third-and-18. Just because the man is down does not mean we cannot kick him."

Amid the fallout, Heimerdinger was a hasty hire made by the Jets from the Tennessee Titans. During his tenure there, quarterback Steve McNair set a personal career best Quarterback Rating (103.4) and the Titans had been to the Super Bowl, scoring as many as 26 points per game when McNair had been healthy for a full season. Jets fans were infatuated with the difference in how the offensive grass grew on the other side of the fence.

But the Jets' head coach Herman Edwards had hired Hackett for sound reasons. Hackett specialized in installing and employing a West Coast offense: a low-risk attack with running as its backbone, supplemented with short, well-timed passes designed for a high completion rate and yards gained after the catch. In 2004, the Jets lost fewer fumbles than any other NFL team. They had logged a staggering 199 offensive plays from scrimmage—about three full games worth of snaps—for every fumble lost. One could say that they took "low-risk" to new highs. Things had meshed very well for this team.

Replacing Hackett's "small-ball" for Heimerdinger's "big-play offense" might eventually evolve into the ability of the Jets to produce more points. But for the present, I propose to Eric, let's draw a parallel here. Suppose it was his police precinct that had been re-armed for more explosiveness. "Instead of carrying the revolvers you've been trained to hold and shoot since police academy," I tell him, "let's say you're in action out on the street, suddenly put on the offensive chasing down bank robbers with long-distance rifles. How much time would you and the other cops need in order to adjust to carrying a different weapon, engaging that weapon, and then aiming it while you're on the run? No cop could go right out into the line of fire and expect to succeed—or avoid disaster—without being completely retrained in the new weaponry, right? Even if you had six weeks of training like the NFL teams get in the summer, the first real action probably wouldn't go smoothly, would it?"

Then I hit him with the clincher. "Heimerdinger and the Chiefs' new defensive coordinator worked on the same team last season."

He gives a grim nod. He understands. The Chiefs' new defensive coordinator was Gunther Cunningham, an ex-head coach of the Chiefs and former defensive coordinator for the Raiders. Cunningham had been employed by Tennessee in 2003 and 2004 as the Titans' linebackers coach. Although "only" a position coach for the Titans, Cunningham was certainly an overqualified position coach, one whose linebackers went up against Heimerdinger's offensive plays every day in practice for two seasons.

Cunningham, and many of his players on the Kansas City defense, would know the Jets' newest offensive plays—and very possibly some of New York's sideline and line of scrimmage calls—as well as anyone on the Jets would.

But at the point when he should be conceding to this superior insight, something instinctive within Straight-Up Fan is compelled to battle back. "Yeah, but it works both ways," Eric says. "The Jets might know what the Chiefs will do on defense. Plus, our defense is better than their defense, especially against the run, and the Chiefs won't stop Curtis Martin's running."

After starting on 180-degree opposite sides, he had been right there with me for a few minutes. But Straight-Up Fan is conditioned to yield to his fantasies. I make a last-ditch attempt at rescuing him. First, by explaining how the

Jets' 2005 defense appeared better than it really was by virtue of having played the second-weakest 2004 offensive rushing schedule in the NFL. By contrast, that "overrated" defense would be facing the best rushing offense next Sunday. A new season, which starts against a more powerful opponent than they had faced on balance a year ago, would be grounds for reassessment of that New York defense.

This goes in one ear and out the other. So does a warning about how total chaos could envelop the normally in-control Jets if the Chiefs—with that 30 points-per-game offense—should make a couple of quick, early scores to take a 10-0, 13-0 or 14-0 lead. In that instance, the Jets—a team whose entire being had been geared to grinding out leads and protecting them—would be attempting to come from behind. The old Jets' way—grinding it out on the ground—becomes less effective when a team is trailing and the clock is ticking against them. The new Jets' way—with more high-risk plays being executed live for the first time and under the extraordinary duress of a deficit—would increase the potential for screw-ups in an already negative-expectation situation. In other words, the Jets had two choices, and each of them would amount to digging their own grave.

• • •

Straight-Up Man

Straight-Up Man wants a personally satisfying result in an "entertainment only" involvement. Negative possibilities—often a foregone conclusion—are blocked out. Clings desperately to hope for a happy ending. In the event of disappointing result, will seek to assign blame for it within the ranks of his team, or the referees. Also known as Straight-Up Fan or Straight-Up American.

ATS Man

ATS Man wants to make money. Because every game is a potential opportunity, he must establish a clear, objective focus for the purpose of making a confident projection based on the relative merits of the situation. When the elements in place are understood and the focus is unbiased, the future becomes easier to predict.

Ultimately, despite the failure to change Straight-Up Man's viewpoint, ATS Man gained something from the discussion: more confidence. Nothing Eric said convinced me that the Jets had a legitimate chance to overcome:

• Historical odds against NFL road team.
• Learning curve in new offensive system.
• Learning curve in new offensive system in first crack at it.

- Learning curve in new offensive system in first crack at it, vs. opposing defensive coordinator who was an eyewitness to it for two seasons.
- Their own overrated defense.

For wagering purposes, the margin of error on the New York side was slim: only +3 points. Seven days out, to me—and others like me—the future looked like this:

Best Bet

KANSAS CITY over NY JETS by 14

Herman's Head heard voices that told him to get a new man from Tennessee to coordinate the Jetsons' offense. But isn't a head coach supposed to be his own guy? Herman forgets that Jets fans, whiny about the old offense, wear hard hats over thick skulls that contain no concept of what might happen initially when there is deviation from a blueprint. KANSAS CITY, 34-20.-*Sports Reporter, Vol. 30, Issue 2: September 4*, 2005.

A week later, on Opening Day, ATS Men across America are already looking ahead to NFL games that will take place in Weeks 3 and 4, because they have already targeted potential Week 2 opportunities.

Kansas City's eventual 20-point winning margin vs. the Jets actually made the game a bigger rout than the *Sports Reporter* projection had called for. For wagering purposes against the spread, the Jets would have needed +21 points—3 touchdowns—to cover it!

Amid all the old news, er, post-game reports that seized upon how the Jets-Chiefs matchup played against popular expectations raised by past performances, I'm thinking two things: a) "Tell me something I didn't already know." b) "They should all be this easy."

At that point, the Labor Day conversation with Eric was the furthest thing from my mind because it was never about his opinion vs. mine. Straight-Up Man's insights mean very little to an ATS Man, with one key exception: Straight-Up Men inhabit ATS World, which is a very segregated place. Any regular fan who enjoys the lure of gambling—Eric not being one of them—is welcome to back his opinions with money in ATS World. But the catch is that Straight-Up Man—in his non-evolved state—is not destined to thrive in ATS World. ATS Man really has to stick to the great American work ethic for his best chance at making it there. Before you make the move to ATS World, you must first rip away your Straight-Up roots. You don't bring opinions from Straight-Up America into ATS World, because in a suitcase that needs to be stocked with instruments and tools that help you predict what tends to happen, opinions sure waste a lot of space.

2

NFL Infrastructure

I **F YOU LOVE** playing in office pools, on parlay cards, or have been fortunate enough to take trips to Las Vegas to spend NFL Sundays in the sports books, it is sometimes hard to fathom that all of this sweet, NFL action from 1 p.m. Eastern to 12 a.m. Eastern—then again on Monday Night if so desired—was not established to fill the slots on the sheet, the ticket, or the big board so that we could all try to leverage our viewing time for fun and profit.

But that was not the case. Their game came first. Our game is the by-product of their game's shelf-life for pure rooting interests—which eventually are put away as childish things. The offshoot is now a game of its own, the game within the game that takes place outside the game. Strange, isn't it?

According to *Forbes* magazine, the National Football League is the world's most valuable and profitable team sport. It enjoys the highest per-game attendance of any professional sports league in the world; in 2006, more than 67,000 seats per game were sold. The average team was worth $733 million in that year, which was a 17 percent increase from the previous year. Operating income for the 32 teams was $851 million on revenue of $5.3 billion.

In 2007, the contracts negotiated by the NFL with CBS, NBC, FOX, ESPN, and its own NFL Network accounted for a combined total of $3.1 billion per year for the broadcast rights.

All 50 or so players on every NFL team are union members. The National Football League Players Association negotiates the general minimum contract-called the Collective Bargaining Agreement—for all players in the league. The Collective Bargaining Agreement establishes a minimum salary for its players.

Players are tiered into three different levels with regards to their rights to negotiate for contracts: a) Draftees, b) players with three to five full seasons in the NFL who are playing with expired contracts (Restricted Free Agents), and c) players with five or more full seasons in the NFL who are playing with expired contracts (Unrestricted Free Agents).

Years	Minimum Salary
0:	$50,000
1:	$360,000
2:	$435,000
3:	$510,000
4-6:	$595,000
7-9:	$720,000
10+:	$820,000

FIGURE 2-1

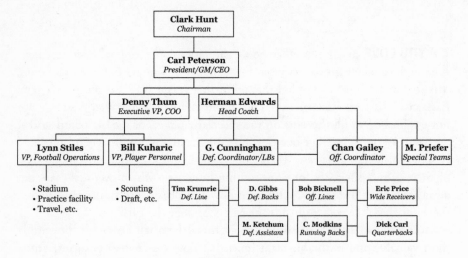

FIGURE 2-2

Most NFL owners choose to run their teams similarly to the typical U.S. corporation. The head coach can be considered as a Chief Operating Officer and the General Manager a Chief Executive Officer.

Head Coaches—the beleaguered men who answer the same stupid questions in the same evasive fashion before and after games and get more television face time than any single face-masked player—are becoming superstars on the pay scale. According to the *New York Post*, NFL head coach salaries were growing five times as fast as players' paychecks as the 2007 season began, with the average annual head coach salary having more than tripled to $3.25 million since 1997.

Ironically, when it comes to salaries, these unionized players and non-union head coaches can negotiate as independent contractors. Isn't that special? They employ agents who negotiate with franchise management for higher salaries. As of the 2005 NFL season, the highest-paid player was Atlanta Falcons quarterback

Michael Vick, with an overall contract value of 10 years at $130 million, averaging $13 million a year, including signing bonuses and annual salary. At the time of this book's publication, Vick was in federal prison for being a ringleader in the world of illegal dogfighting. Michael Vick is not a very bright fellow, nor are many of his NFL ball-playing brethren.

This perceived lack of socially redeeming qualities in its most talented performers is one reason that people like to bet on NFL game outcomes, and not necessarily carry a devoted, fanatical rooting attachment to individual players or teams. After all, these players and coaches are getting paid whether they win or lose, and rarely if ever take a cut in pay. When they lose, they can laugh all the way to the bank. "These clowns are making millions off the public," thinks the point-spread player. "I'm gonna try to make some money back off them."

Bravo.

•   •   •

BUT YOU CAN never forget the one absolute truth that hovers over the NFL and those who wager on it, which is the existence of a fundamental difference between "Straight-Up" and "Against the Spread." Because NFL teams operate in Straight-Up Land with a certain set of objectives and an ultimate goal, they are concerned with scoring one more point than the other guy on a weekly basis. If they can win by a bigger margin than one point, they'll take it. If not, they're fine with it. The NFL bettor, on the other hand, must win by at least one point against the spread. When your team is not playing the same game as you, there is a world of difference between the two.

As the NFL has evolved, some might argue—validly—that it has become a harder sport to beat vs. the points. The NFL has historically inserted checks and balances into its overall process for the sake of more contentious games. More contentious Sundays create the most interesting highlight shows and the longest possible reaction and exposure into the next weekend's games, where the cycle repeats itself. Unlike Major League Baseball, where the wealthiest owners are often in the post-season, parity rules the NFL. Because a short, 16-game regular season minimizes the chance of great comebacks in the standings, fairness and grading curves are important to the NFL.

The Draft

To maintain the smallest gap possible between the best team and the worst team, the annual draft of college players is held in reverse order of finish. Worst drafts first, first drafts worst. Teams can and often do trade draft picks.

Six Divisions

An NFL team need only beat out three other teams to win its division and automatically qualify for the playoffs. Think about it. When an NFL team beats three other teams, that team has "earned" the right to call itself a "champion." Championships come cheap, don't they?

The Schedule

In another nod to fairness, teams within a division play 14 common opponents in the 16-game regular season schedule: The other three in their division twice—home and away, to be fair; all four teams from another division in their conference, to be fair; all four teams from a division in the other conference, to be fair. The two remaining games are assigned based on the teams' records from the previous season. Best records are matched up with best records. For instance, the year after winning the Super Bowl, the 2007 Indianapolis Colts were assigned New England (14 wins—including post-season—in '06, 18 the next) and Baltimore (13 wins in '06, 5 the next). Their division rivals were placed along the grading curve to help get them up to Indianapolis' level, or bring Indianapolis down to their level, or both. Houston got Miami (6 wins in '06, 1 the next) and Cleveland (4 wins, 10 the next). Tennessee got Cincinnati (8, 7) and the New York Jets (10, 4). Jacksonville got Buffalo (7, 7) and Pittsburgh (8, 10). After seventeen weeks of competition on the curve, the Colts withstood the parity plan well enough: 13 wins, vs. 11-10-8 for Jacksonville, Tennessee, and Houston, respectively. But following a season of 12-8-8-6 wins in that division in 2006, you can see that the parity plan helped to elevate the three teams behind them. How much more time in the sun does Indianapolis have remaining?

Wild Cards

If a team finds itself mathematically eliminated from the division title at a certain point in the season, not to worry. There is always the wild card slot to claim as their ticket to play in the post-season. As any serious poker player knows, wild cards make it harder for the sharp player to win when matched up against less sophisticated opponents.

The introduction of wild cards into the AFC and NFC increased the length of competitiveness within the NFL season and created fewer non-goal oriented spots in the schedule. When there are more games between teams that are trying their hardest to achieve attainable goals, it makes the challenge of predicting a winner more difficult. Coaches don't start playing for next year until a wild card spot is officially out of reach. After seven games in 2005, the

Baltimore Ravens were 2-5, had virtually no chance to win the AFC North, and it was calculated that they would have to win eight of nine games just to get a wild card berth. "We would have to get on a heck of a run," head coach Brian Billick told the *Baltimore Sun* at the time. "We're cognizant of that. Until someone tells us that mathematically it isn't going to happen, that's the hook you have to hold onto. That's where you generate your enthusiasm. Why give up on that hope?" (The Ravens finished 6-10 that year and well out of the wild card running.)

In the 2007 season, after 11 of the 16 regular season games had been played, Green Bay and Dallas each had records of 10-1. With five games still to play, the Packers and Cowboys were nevertheless virtual cinches to win their respective NFC North and East divisions because Dallas had a three-game lead and a season sweep of 7-4 NFC East rival New York, while the Packers had a four-game lead in the North on 6-5 second-place Detroit. Had there been only three divisions in each conference—as there had been from 1970 to 2002—only one NFC division title race would have existed during the course of those final five weeks. With a minimum number of goals being chased to create fan interest, television ratings and live attendance would drop. But the way the system has been arranged, there was still plenty of division-title chasing taking place in the South and West, plus wild card activity that would leave races unsettled until the last weekend, as is almost always the case.

The Schedule, Part II

When NFL coaches began dealing with the four-division set-up, they realized that division games were like a late-season baseball series between the Yankees and Red Sox when those rivals are separated by only a few games in the standings—like nearly every NFL team is at any given point of the season. Those games are worth two games, and head coaches have learned to prioritize them—especially the divisional home games. For instance, if the 6-3 team beats the 5-4 team it will be 7-3 vs. 5-5, but if they lose, they are tied at 6-4. Aha! Because these division rivalry games are so important in the grand goal scheme, coaches made a request to the NFL that the league group division games together more frequently instead of sandwiching them between non-division or non-conference games. By attacking the schedule in more classified groups instead of darting from inter-division to intra-division to non-conference to intra-division, etc., it makes it easier for coaches to manage bodies and prepare against their given goals. Whenever two opposing coaches are getting the same relief to facilitate the task, it becomes harder to pick the winner vs. the spread.

• • •

THE MOUNTING CHALLENGES to winning vs. the spread only makes ATS Man more determined to uncover new and useful indicators in his attempt to master his craft and make a profit. The coaches have worked long and hard for the right to take the easiest way out. That's why they sit on leads and fall on the football and let the clock run out in the final 90 seconds instead of lining up and playing. ATS Man can pass on a game, which is the equivalent to the quarterback taking a knee. But if he wants to win, then he has to make the commitment to prepare like Bill Belichick, the genius head coach of the New England Patriots. Before he reached four Super Bowls and won three with the Pats, Belichick made Bill Parcells look smarter than Parcells ever was or will be by working together with his Giants' offensive coordinator Ron Erhardt to devise game plans that won post-season games against Hall of Fame quarterbacks John Elway (1986 Super Bowl), Joe Montana (1990 NFC Championship Game), and Jim Kelly (1990 Super Bowl).

The best head coaches work and work and work and work until they figure out how to minimize the other team's strengths. The NFL has that ever-present strength of parity at play every weekend. Inevitably, parity causes the least tenacious observers to punch the wall and declare in moments of frustration-usually after an "unpredictable" upset has caused an investment loss, "The NFL is impossible to predict!"

The NFL is not unpredictable. But to get the best possible grasp of it, you have to be patient, ask questions, dig for answers, and, when you get tired of digging, dig deeper.

3
Understanding Statistics and Rankings

IN ATTEMPTING TO solve NFL point-spread mysteries, you'll come across a lot of statistics: individual and team, per game, and per season. The NFL is up to its shoulder pads in statistics, and all the numbers mean different things to different people. Agents use them to negotiate player contracts. Players use them to complain about not playing or not carrying the ball or catching passes, because they think it hurts their bargaining power for the next contract. Coaches use them to determine strengths and weaknesses of opponents as well as their own team. The football media uses them as facts that help differentiate between stories about how one NFL team beats another NFL team—which happens 16 times every weekend. Sometimes, those facts get in the way of the real story as far as the bettor is concerned:

San Francisco, CA (Sports Network)—Marc Bulger completed 21 of 32 passes for 155 yards and the only touchdown in the game, helping lead the St. Louis Rams to a 13-9 win over the San Francisco 49ers.

Bulger was averaging about 260 yards passing per game in his career prior to that game. The 155 passing yards was drastically lower than average, among the lowest single-game outputs in his career. Yet St. Louis (−3) won and covered. Why?

Irving, TX (Sports Network)—Tony Romo tossed 4 touchdown passes to Terrell Owens, as the Dallas Cowboys slipped past the Washington Redskins, 28-23, at Texas Stadium.

Four touchdown passes is the stuff of an all-star, a quarterback who dates actresses and sees other actresses on the side. You'd think that a point-spread cover would have accompanied four scores by the Dallas Cowboys' high-profile quarterback-to-wide receiver connection. But it did not. Why not?

They do a lot of reporting and reacting, but newspaper and television recaps don't necessarily give a lot of answers. The box scores and gamebooks stored on web sites like nfl.com and espn.com are silent, but they hold a lot more clues as to why an individual result occurred as it did. However, since individual results by themselves do not serve as indicators for the next result for either side, ATS Man needs to understand overall statistics and averages to help predict the future. At the same time, ATS Man needs to understand that the coaches are using the same statistics and averages—whether they are good, bad, or medio-cre—to help overcome a weakness or to help attack an opposing weakness.

Almost all NFL numbers need to be framed in the proper context to help prioritize their significance, and to tune them out when necessary. The typical report tends to sensationalize the normal and the underwhelming, like Marc Bulger's completing of 21 of 32 passes for 155 yards and one touchdown.

Table 3-1 helps display the range of NFL performance possibilities by show-ing the two highest, two lowest, and medians in nine different team offensive categories over a five-season period. (Medians, which are the middle, can be better measurements than averages because averages can be skewed by severe highs and lows.

Bulger's 21-for-32 passing afternoon was just slightly better than the median completion percentage. But the 155 passing yards created a YPA of 4.8, which, sustained over the course of a season, would have been a record low. Yet Bulger was highlighted at the very top of the story. Almost as ironi-cally, his team covered the spread! Obviously, the main reasons for St. Louis's win and cover were elsewhere amid the sea of statistics. In this particular instance, most of the reasons involved San Francisco simply being worse in several areas, including turnovers. In hindsight (or, as a before-the-fact omen for some ATS Men), covering despite so many sub-par readings on the

NFL 2003-'07 Rush & Pass	RA	RY	RYPC	PC	PA	PY	Comp%	YPA	Yds Sacked
NFL High	34	183	5.4	27	41	298	68.4%	8.2	26
2nd Highest	33	161	5.1	26	40	294	67.9%	8.2	26
MEDIAN	27	111	3.9	19	32	217	60.2%	6.7	13
2nd Fewest	21	71	3.1	13	24	137	52.3%	5.3	5
NFL Fewest	19	70	3.0	12	23	136	50.7%	5.3	5

FIGURE 3-1

statistical scale was the foreshadowing for St. Louis's closing out the rest of the season at 2-4 ATS.

When too much of the advance talk about an NFL matchup is how one of the teams ranks last in a certain category, it's easy to get all hung up over it and put too much targeted focus on it, while overlooking something else that might be a problem for the other side. Within a month in 2007, the Pittsburgh Steelers played road games at Denver and at the New York Jets. At the time, each opponent ranked last in rushing defense in the NFL. A typical NFL media report:

> ". . . San Diego piled up 214 yards on the ground against a Denver defense that ranks last in the NFL defending the run and has been trampled in each of its last three games. The Broncos yielded 226 rushing yards to Indianapolis the previous week, and 186 to Jacksonville in a 23-14 home loss on September 23 . . . Denver could have similar problems this Sunday, since the Steelers own the league's second-best ground attack and speedy running back Willie Parker has gone for over 100 yards in four of the team's five games. Pittsburgh has won all four of those contests . . ."

Blah, blah, blah. The Broncos were in the early stages of playing a new defensive system while allowing lots of rushing yards. Off a bye week, they were able to progress along the learning curve. Pittsburgh was a –3 favorite on the road, and we've already determined that road teams lose six of every ten games in the NFL. When this particular game was completed, the Steelers had rushed only 26 times for 119 yards—NFL median range. By being able to generate 21 first downs with their own offense (greater than the NFL median of 18.5), and improving slightly on defense, the Broncos were able to win the game "despite" having the "worst" run defense in the NFL. Remember, it's a team game.

2003-'07 NFL OFFENSE	Pts/ G	Plays/ G	Yds/ G	Yds/ Ply	1st/ G	3rd %	Pen PG	Pen Yd/ G	TOP	Fum	Lost	TO
NFL Best	36.8	68.1	418	6.7	24.9	56%	3.7	27	34:04	12	4	24
2nd Best	32.6	67.8	411	6.4	24.6	52%	3.9	30	34:00	13	5	24
NFL MEDIAN	20.5	62.7	322	5.1	18.5	39%	6.5	54	31:15	25	12	0
2nd Worst	13.2	56.0	237	4.1	13.6	25%	8.9	71	26:47	42	22	–24
NFL Worst	10.5	54.1	224	3.9	11.9	24%	9.1	74	26:47	42	26	–24

FIGURE 3-2

When the offensive unit is able to stay on the field, it can protect the shaky run defense. When the offense is on the field and also scoring points, it can force the opponent to throw against the poor run defense, which bypasses the perceived matchup advantage that everyone who believes what they read is focused on before the game begins. The opponent can always try to run while it trails and continue to exploit the matchup, but there is a little detail called the 60-minute game clock—it winds down faster with an overabundance of running plays and is always ticking towards expiration.

They say that the essence of mathematics is not to make simple things complicated, but to make complicated things simple. Eventually, being inundated by numbers might prompt you to create some new measurements on your own that aren't generally reported. But that's for a later chapter or two. In the meantime, do not sell yourself out to statistics and rankings without carefully considering what they might be concealing.

4

Understanding the NFL Landscape

LET'S GET SOMETHING straight right now. Anyone going into an NFL season expecting everything to play out about the same as it did the year before should not be wagering on these games. One of the rules heading into every NFL season should be to challenge the status quo, to avoid the path followed by members of Straight-Up World.

It would have been very easy, and would have required very little effort, to assume that because the 2005 Tampa Bay Buccaneers had won 11 games and were returning 21 starters in 2006, that they would have once again been a "good" team in 2006. But who is to say that just because the Bucs won 11 games in 2005 and made the playoffs, that Tampa Bay was actually a "good" team that season? Remember, you have to challenge every contention that a number or a statistic might imply before conceding that there could be truth in it.

Personally, I thought that in 2005, Tampa Bay had been luckier than Luciano in encountering a string of sorry-ass opponents that were experiencing nothing but bad luck of their own in 2005. A detailed outline to support that contention was presented in *Sports Reporter*'s *2006 Zone Blitz*. It was called "10 Things to Hate About the Bucs" leading into the 2006 season:

1. Played the second-weakest schedule in the 2005 NFL season.
2. Managed to build an 11-5 SU record and win a division despite a differential of less than one point in their PF/PA per game averages.
3. Because their O-line can't protect any of its quarterbacks, they employ a third-year player, second-season starter [Chris Simms], whose college team [Texas] rose up and won the national championship the season after he left, and whose father was an oft-injured NFL bust at the position until his sixth season in the league—when he was finally surrounded by the best offensive line, and the best defense.
4. After back-to-back seasons where the offense averaged 5.3 and 5.2 yards per play, it regressed down to 4.8 yards per play in 2005.

5. That offense ranked 25th in first downs per game, at 16.8, between the directionless offenses of Buffalo and Miami.
6. The only good season in the tenure of "offensive-minded" head coach Jon Gruden came when the defense carried them with 7 TDs and monster pressure.
7. Had so little weaponry on offense that they had to use a rookie running back [Cadillac Williams] full tilt in the first three games of his NFL career, after which he got a sore hamstring that he nursed through the rest of the season.
8. Bucs were one of only two teams in Top 10 of TO Ratio that lost money vs. the spread.
9. So many free-agent pick-ups and departures the last several seasons, yet so little overall performance change.
10. Projected offensive line re-shuffling includes two rookies, and an import from Dallas—one of the weakest NFL lines in '05. Defense returns another year older, mostly status quo, without longtime DL coach and assistant head coach Rod Marinelli, now head coach in Detroit.

This quote from Tampa Bay's veteran linebacker Derrick Brooks only solidified my anti-Bucs position:

"I think our off-season was real big in keeping 21 of the 22 guys that started. To us, that was our key acquisitions, keeping everybody together and continuing to build on it."

What did Derrick Brooks know? He was only a player. All players think that they are about to set the world on fire! Inhabitants of ATS World—forecasters—tend to know more than some linebacker as far as anticipating which direction the Tampa Bay Buccaneers would go in 2006!

The real fact of the matter is that since 1995, an average of eleven teams per NFL regular season have either progressed or regressed by from 4 to 9 wins from the season prior. Four games is 25 percent of the schedule, in a league where one win—6 percent of the schedule—can be the difference between making the playoffs and making plans with Vegas hookers (hey, the "golf course" thing went out the window a long time ago).

In a given season, the win totals of eight to fifteen NFL teams will rise or fall by at least four games. Since 1995, the four-game minimum change in either direction has occurred in 128 out of a possible 345 teams, 37.1 percent of all possible instances. If you don't believe it, you can identify them all on the accompanying Figure 4-1.

Anyone who had examined the quarterbacks that Tampa Bay had faced in 2005 would have agreed that there have been many greater challenges presented to teams in the history of the NFL. The list of quarterbacks that opposed the Bucs included these guys, with my own notes:

Week 1:   Daunte Culpepper pulled a classic Daunte, making 5 turnovers.
Week 2:   First NFL career road start for Buffalo QB J.P. Losman.
Week 3:   Ripken-Favre and the Slacker Packers!
Week 4:   Joey Harrington and the sad-sack Lions.
Week 5:   Vinny Testaverde and the sad-sack Jets . . . and Tampa lost!
Week 7:   Sorry-asses Alex Smith and Cody Pickett of San Francisco . . . and Tampa lost!
Weeks 9-11: Faced competent veteran QBs leading competent opponents and allowed 34, 35 and 27 points.
Week 12:   Rookie QB Kyle Orton of the Bears . . . and they lost!
Week 13:   Aaron (Which Way is the Goal Line?) Brooks and the soulless Saints.

When the 2005 regular season was complete, Tampa Bay's defense had produced a very "solid" Opposing Quarterback Rating of 73.5. And why not? Look at who they were facing! For 2006, that same defense—which had returned just about "everyone"—eventually produced the league's fourth-worst Opposing Quarterback Rating for the season, 91.0.

Tampa Bay's eventual –7 win regression from 2005 was taking place as New Orleans, Baltimore, and the New York Jets were gaining 7, 7, and 6 wins from the prior season. Naturally, Tampa Bay would eventually represent a net loss vs. the spread on a game-by-game basis that season, while Baltimore, New Orleans, and the Jets were among the strongest net profit sides of 2006.

To really understand the NFL and how it works, you have to attempt to develop an understanding for why a team's body of work in a given season may have been facilitated by circumstances that are unlikely to be duplicated the next time they launch a trip through the schedule. In other words, take that 2005-to-2006 Tampa Bay research, analysis, and projection and multiply it by 32. That's how hard you have to work at it.

· · ·

WHEN 2005 HAD ended, that Tampa Bay team was completing its third straight season of sub-average points scored (see Table 4.2), which was yet another reason to doubt their ability to sustain the 11-5 record. It was common knowledge they were going with most of the same players. Therefore, it was very reasonable to ask: "Hey, where are more points going to come from?"

The widest gap from high average to low average was 24.6 points in 1998, from Minnesota (34.7) down to Philadelphia (10.1). League-wide, the average

SU Wins	1996	1997	1998	1999	2000	2001	2002	2003	2004	2005	2006	2007
Arizona	7	4	9	6	3	7	5	4	6	5	5	8
Atlanta	3	7	14	5	4	7	9	5	11	8	7	4
Baltimore	4	6	6	8	12	10	7	11	9	6	13	5
Buffalo	10	6	10	11	8	3	8	7	9	5	7	7
Carolina	12	7	4	8	7	1	7	11	7	11	8	7
Chicago	7	4	4	6	5	13	4	7	5	11	13	7
Cincinnati	8	7	3	4	4	6	2	8	8	11	8	7
Cleveland				2	3	7	9	5	4	6	4	10
Dallas	10	6	10	8	5	5	5	10	6	9	9	13
Denver	13	12	14	6	11	8	9	10	10	13	9	7
Detroit	5	9	5	8	9	2	3	5	6	5	3	7
Green Bay	13	13	11	8	9	12	12	10	10	4	8	13
Houston							4	4	7	2	6	8
Indianapolis	9	3	3	13	10	6	10	12	12	14	12	13
Jacksonville	9	11	11	14	7	6	6	5	9	12	8	11
Kansas City	9	13	7	9	7	6	8	13	7	10	9	4
Miami	8	9	10	9	11	11	9	10	4	9	6	1
Minnesota	9	9	15	10	11	5	6	9	8	9	6	8
New England	11	10	9	8	5	11	9	14	14	10	12	16

New Orleans	3	6	6	3	10	7	9	8	8	3	10	7
NY Giants	6	10	8	7	12	7	10	4	6	11	8	10
NY Jets	1	9	12	8	9	10	9	6	10	4	10	4
Oakland	7	4	8	8	12	10	11	4	5	4	2	4
Philadelphia	10	6	3	5	11	11	12	12	13	6	10	8
Pittsburgh	10	11	7	6	9	13	10	6	15	11	8	10
San Diego	8	4	5	8	1	5	8	4	12	9	14	11
San Francisco	12	13	12	4	6	12	10	7	2	4	7	5
Seattle	7	8	8	9	6	9	7	10	9	13	9	10
St. Louis	6	5	4	13	10	14	7	11	8	6	8	3
Tampa Bay	6	10	8	11	10	9	12	7	5	11	4	9
Tennessee	8	8	8	13	13	7	11	12	5	4	8	10
Washington	9	8	6	10	8	8	7	5	6	10	5	9
> = + / –4 Wins	—	12	10	10	8	15	7	14	11	15	13	13

FIGURE 4-1

year-to-year change in points scored per team is about 3.4 points. Knowledge of this valid trend sets you up to red-flag teams with drastic increases for deeper investigation on why the spikes occurred, and whether or not a "correction" is due the following season based on changes within the team, their opponents, the schedule situations, or just plain luck due to change course.

Anytime you see a number that is more than twice the size of the Standard Deviation, you can be pretty sure that the number is coming down the next chance it gets. Dozen-year Standard Deviations in average Points For (PF) game per team are listed in the far right column of Table 4-2.

Time out!

Oh, intimidated by the phrase "Standard Deviation," eh? Stubbornly convinced that something like a Standard Deviation is over your head, too complicated to understand, and a waste of your time, eh? You want to be a wise guy and keep trying to predict the outcome of NFL games without background knowledge of Standard Deviations, one of the most important measurements in the field of probability and statistics, eh?

Well, suck it up, wise guy! That kind of thinking gets quarterbacks demoted; when they quit on themselves attempting to learn the offense! Standard Deviation—which measures the spread of numbers in a set of data—can be automatically calculated with a few mouse clicks by anyone with a PC and a Microsoft Excel spreadsheet. Try it. Learn something new. It might open your eyes!

Start with those 1998 Minnesota Vikings first. Their average points per game jumped by 9.1 from the season prior. (Back then, Minnesota's eleven-year Standard Deviation was less than the 4.8, so 9.1 was more than twice the Standard Deviation.) The inevitable regression that occurred in 1999 was to an average level that many teams would love to sport: 25.7 points per game. Heck, until 2007, the Arizona Cardinals hadn't averaged more than 20 points per game in a season since Moby Dick was a minnow! But a regression to 25.7 points per game for that particular edition of the Minnesota Vikings ultimately led to a 1999 point-spread record of 5-11 ATS even though they finished 10-6 and made the playoffs.

Playoffs? Who said anything about playoffs?! We're just trying to win some games against the spread here!

The 2006 New Orleans Saints and 2006 Chicago Bears increased their Points For per game by 10.4 and 11.4. Guess who dropped to 7-9 ATS and 6-10 ATS after having been 10-6 ATS apiece the season before? Guess who didn't make the playoffs a year after competing against each other in the 2006 NFC Championship Game? That's right, the 2007 Chicago Bears and the 2007 New Orleans Saints!

Even slightly lesser spikes should serve as a signal to raise at least a yellow caution flag and view a team with skepticism as it enters the next season with last

Avg PF	1996	1997	1998	1999	2000	2001	2002	2003	2004	2005	2006	2007	StD
Arizona	18.8	17.7	20.3	15.3	13.1	18.4	16.4	13.9	17.8	19.4	19.6	25.3	3.2
Atlanta	19.3	20.0	27.6	17.8	15.8	18.2	25.1	18.7	21.3	21.9	18.3	16.2	3.5
Baltimore	23.2	20.4	16.8	20.3	20.8	18.9	19.8	25.3	19.8	16.6	22.1	17.2	2.6
Buffalo	19.9	15.9	25.0	20.0	19.7	16.6	23.7	15.3	24.7	16.9	18.8	15.8	3.5
Carolina	22.9	16.6	**21.0**	**26.3**	**19.4**	15.8	16.1	20.1	22.2	24.4	16.9	16.8	3.6
Chicago	17.7	16.4	17.3	17.0	13.5	**21.1**	**17.6**	17.7	**14.4**	**16.3**	**26.7**	**20.9**	3.5
Cincinnati	23.3	22.2	16.8	17.7	11.6	14.1	17.4	21.6	23.2	26.3	23.3	23.8	4.5
Cleveland				13.6	10.1	17.8	21.5	15.9	17.3	14.5	14.9	25.1	4.4
Dallas	17.9	19.0	23.8	22.0	18.4	15.4	13.6	18.1	18.3	20.3	26.6	28.4	4.4
Denver	24.4	29.5	31.3	**19.6**	**30.3**	**21.3**	24.5	23.8	23.8	24.7	19.9	20.0	4.1
Detroit	18.9	23.7	19.1	20.1	19.2	16.9	19.1	16.9	18.5	14.9	19.1	21.6	2.3
Green Bay	28.5	26.4	25.5	22.3	22.1	24.4	24.9	27.6	26.5	18.6	18.4	27.2	3.3
Houston							13.3	15.8	19.3	16.3	16.7	23.7	3.6
Indianapolis	19.8	19.6	19.4	26.4	26.8	25.8	21.8	27.9	32.6	27.4	26.7	28.1	4.1
Jacksonville	20.3	24.6	24.5	24.8	22.9	18.4	20.5	17.3	16.3	22.6	23.2	25.3	3.1

(Continued)

Figure 4-2 *(Continued)*

Avg PF	1996	1997	1998	1999	2000	2001	2002	2003	2004	2005	2006	2007	StD
Kansas City	18.6	23.4	20.4	24.4	22.2	20.0	29.2	30.3	30.2	25.3	20.7	14.1	4.9
Miami	21.2	21.2	20.1	20.4	20.2	21.5	23.6	19.4	17.0	19.8	16.3	16.7	2.2
Minnesota	18.6	22.1	34.8	24.9	24.8	18.1	24.4	26.0	25.3	19.1	17.4	22.8	4.8
New England	26.1	23.1	21.1	18.7	17.3	23.2	23.8	21.8	27.3	23.7	24.1	36.8	4.9
New Orleans	14.3	14.8	19.1	16.3	22.1	20.8	27.0	21.3	21.8	14.7	25.8	22.4	4.3
NY Giants	15.1	19.2	17.9	18.7	20.5	18.4	19.8	15.2	18.5	26.4	22.2	23.3	3.2
NY Jets	17.4	21.8	26.0	19.3	20.1	19.3	22.4	17.7	20.8	15.0	19.8	16.8	2.9
Oakland	21.3	20.3	18.0	24.4	29.9	24.9	28.1	16.9	20.0	18.1	10.5	17.7	5.3
Philadelphia	22.7	19.8	10.1	17.0	21.9	21.4	26.1	23.4	24.1	19.4	24.9	21.0	4.3
Pittsburgh	21.5	23.3	16.4	19.8	20.1	22.0	24.4	18.8	23.3	24.3	22.1	24.6	2.5
San Diego	19.4	16.6	15.1	16.8	16.8	20.8	20.8	19.6	27.9	26.1	30.8	25.8	5.1
San Francisco	24.9	23.4	29.9	18.4	24.3	25.6	22.9	24.0	16.2	14.9	18.6	13.7	4.9
Seattle	19.8	22.8	23.3	21.1	20.0	18.8	22.2	25.3	23.2	27.6	20.9	24.6	2.5
St. Louis	18.9	18.7	17.8	32.9	33.8	31.4	19.8	27.3	19.9	22.7	22.9	16.4	6.2
Tampa Bay	13.8	18.7	19.6	16.9	24.3	20.3	21.6	18.8	18.8	18.8	13.2	20.9	3.1
Tennessee	21.6	20.8	20.6	24.5	21.6	21.0	22.9	27.2	21.5	18.7	20.3	18.8	2.4
Washington	22.8	20.4	19.9	27.7	17.6	16.0	19.2	17.9	15.0	21.1	19.2	20.9	3.3

FIGURE 4-2

year on the public's mind. The 2000 Carolina Panthers improved their points per game by 5.3 points from the 1999 average, when the record was 8-8 SU, 10-6 ATS. This is what *Sports Illustrated* had to say about the Panthers in August 2000:

"After rallying to an 8-8 finish a year ago, Carolina missed the post-season only by tiebreakers. Truth be told, no one really wanted to play the Panthers in the playoffs. They were scoring points and coming together as a team. Dallas and Detroit, the two 8-8s that made the post-season, were much safer foes. Offensively the Panthers have most of the pieces in place, providing they get another big year from quarterback Steve Beuerlein . . . If Natrone Means and Tshimanga Biakabutuka can combine to get the ground game going, Beuerlein and his receivers proved they can score on anybody . . ."

Another big year from Steve Beuerlein? Who thought that Steve Beuerlein ever had at least one good season? Anyway, when all was said and done the Panthers in the 2000 season that followed would sub-revert to average only 19.4 points per game. The decrease was –6.9 points per game (essentially a full touchdown). Carolina's Straight-Up win count dropped from 8 to 7, but their point-spread cover count dropped from 10 to 7. On a $100 flat-bet basis, 10-6 ATS of 1999 represented 62.5 percent wins and net profit of $340. The 7-9 ATS of 2000 represented 43.8 percent wins and net loss of -$290. The difference between the two performance levels, in terms of dollars, was $630.

The sum of $630 doesn't sound like much. But if you can target just a half-dozen teams destined to regress from one season to the next, then have the courage of your convictions and do a relatively decent job of stepping in against them, you will be poised to win overall when the season is said and done, positioning yourself on the right side of swings that total $3,600 or more. You want to be the guy on the plus side who anticipated change; not the guy on the minus side who began the season by jumping in on last year's hottest teams, and lost.

5

Challenging the General Football Media

BILL PARCELLS SAT slump-shouldered, staring straight ahead during the locker room television press conference. He was dumbstruck at the sequence of events that he himself had just precipitated, and, to his ultimate dismay, was forced to witness.

"I apologize to the people of America."

Based on the doom and gloom being projected on the television screen, you would have thought that the Dallas Cowboys' head coach had either started a war, messed around with an intern, or had irreversibly turned his players into pumpkins at midnight on October 23, 2006.

After his starting quarterback Drew Bledsoe finally threw one interception too many in the first half of an important NFC battle against the New York Giants, Parcells made the big move that observers had been anticipating since exhibition season, the kind of decision that factors into why head coaches are paid the big bucks. He inserted the inexperienced backup quarterback Tony Romo, with the intent to spark the Cowboys in the second half of a game they trailed 12-7 at the half. A high-profile, Monday Night Football game on ESPN between two tried-and-true NFL brand names that was in the process of generating the highest rating of the season for Monday Night Football, and representing the largest audience in the history of cable television at the time—surpassing the 1993 NAFTA debate between H. Ross Perot and Al Gore—ah, look how far we'd come as a nation in thirteen years, eh? An average of 16,028,000 viewers watched the game, whose telecast earned a 12.8 Nielsen rating.

But on his first snap in the third quarter, Romo—oh, the horror—threw an interception. Then he totally deflated the 60,000 Dallas fans in attendance by throwing two more interceptions before the second half ended and the Giants won. As one report said about the new kid, "The mistakes he made with his arm overshadowed anything he did with his feet." The records of division rivals New York and Dallas had each been 3-2 entering the game. When it was over, the Giants were 4-2, Dallas 3-3. A win by Dallas would have reversed their positions, which is why they say that division clashes are worth two games in the standings.

The terrific actor William H. Macy could not have played the role of stunned loser any better than Parcells did in the aftermath of the great letdown. To millions in the record national television audience taking the head coach's words and emotions at face value, he was projecting that he had no clue how to progress from this point on. "I'm ashamed to put a team out there playing like that. They out-everything-ed us. It was a very poor performance."

The *New York Times* led the media's race to pick up the cue the next morning:

IRVING, Tex., Oct. 24-Over the course of a long season, every division sustains tremors. But what happened this week in the National Football Conference East was a seismic shift that vaulted the Giants into first place . . . The loss was viewed locally as one of the most demoralizing in the four-year tenure of Coach Bill Parcells, who is 28-26 in Dallas with one post-season appearance. The loss left the Cowboys in more disarray than their 3-3 record would indicate.

The media sensationalizes almost everything. When it was invented centuries ago, its purpose was to educate and inform the public. To be fair to the *Times*, the story included this quote from Giants' head coach Tom Coughlin:

There's many games to play . . . They're a good football team. They're well coached and they will make the best of whatever they have to. This race is the most difficult one, and I wouldn't speculate on anything except trying to get ourselves ready for the next game.

But that sensible quote from a true insider had no chance of eclipsing the images of what the public had already seen, and would see again in replayed highlights—Bledsoe being sacked, sparking the Giants with the interception, Romo entering midway through to throw gasoline on the fire, and repeated images of Parcells delivering a post-game eulogy. Parcells was the one to blame—the fool for replacing Bledsoe with a spacey kid, and the Cowboys would be divided and confused. Meanwhile, off that one performance, the Dallas defense suddenly couldn't stop "anyone." Never mind that they had only played one opponent that night. And, their loose cannon wide receiver Terrell Owens would be one typical outburst away from completely leveling the house.

The supposed obstacles in front of Dallas in their very next game at the Carolina Panthers were easy to list. Way too easy:

- Short week
- Road game
- Team in disarray
- Romo making first career start

Which, of course, made it the perfect time to be thinking about betting on the Cowboys! You could have refuted all four of the supposed obstacles very quickly:

- Teams have won and/or covered off short weeks in the past.
- They have won and/or covered off short weeks on the road in the past.
- The statement about Dallas being in disarray did not come from Dallas, but from a Straight-Up writer sensationalizing a story for the sake of creating an impact.
- Finally, plenty of NFL teams with first-time starting quarterbacks had either won or covered that particular game. The obscure Randy Fasani of Carolina against the eventual Super Bowl champion Tampa Bay Bucs in 2002 (9-12 loss/cover as +8 underdog), and the high-profile Big Ben Roethlisberger of Pittsburgh in 2004 (13-3 win/cover as +1 underdog at Miami), were only a few of the recent instances.

There was precedent to overcome all four of those points and blow the anti-Dallas case out of the water before it even had a chance to be floated. But the best point to make in support of Dallas, with Romo, against Carolina was never made by anyone in the general sports media, even though the media was already deep into a love affair with a player who was a proven example of why yanking the veteran Bledsoe had a huge upside in the first place.

Only five years earlier, Bledsoe—the very same Drew Bledsoe guy at the center of this very visible current quarterback controversy in Dallas—had, via Week 2 injury, lost his starting job as quarterback of the New England Patriots to a kid named Tom Brady. Bledsoe's 2001 injury occurred in the middle of the Week 2 game against the Jets. After Brady relieved Bledsoe, the Patriots eventually lost the game to a division rival—just as Romo had relieved Bledsoe and Dallas had lost to a division rival. The Patriots were underdogs in the first six games with Brady as the starter, beginning the very next Sunday in his first NFL start against the Indianapolis Colts. How badly did the public overreact to this supposed negative situation for New England? The Colts were the 12-point favorite! New England won the game, 44-13!

Brady's QB Rating of 79.6 for that particular debut start was quite unassuming, certainly not what the public would expect in a game his team won by 31 points. But Brady was one player out of eleven on the offense, and eleven more on the defense, and eleven more on the special teams. They all had a new week of practice after the Bledsoe Interruptus defeat, and Brady and the offense gained the benefit of Brady's practicing with the first unit for the first time—as Romo would be doing prior to his first career start at Carolina.

Eventually the 2001 Patriots won 14 of 16 games started by the inexperienced Brady, the final win being the Super Bowl against the St. Louis Rams as +14 underdogs! New England was 13-2-1 ATS in Brady's starts, 11-2 ATS as underdogs. By Week 12 of that season, Bledsoe had recovered from his injury and was healthy enough to play again. But the Patriots' head coach Bill Belichick refused to make a switch back to Bledsoe because he thought that the raw Brady was his better option at the time. Just like Bill Parcells was deciding now, five years later!

"Dallas, +5 against Carolina" was released as a *Sports Reporter* Midweek Update Best Bet on Friday of that week. For me, any underdog against the Carolina Panthers was going to be attractive. Way back in August, we were on record in *Sports Reporter's Zone Blitz* as being thumbs-down on Carolina as an investment prospect that season. To us, the Panthers were clearly an overvalued team that had benefited from fortunate circumstances and good luck in 2005. The Cowboys, on the other hand, were a talented team making a change; Romo's ability to roll out and throw on the run was the kind of change that causes opposing defensive coordinators to bite their nails. Rollouts confuse defenses because defensive linemen are forced to take a non-traditional route to the quarterback. When that happens, the quarterback buys himself precious time, and only needs to look at half the field. When you give a professional a simplified view and more time to produce, he'll get the job done more often than not if he has a good supporting cast.

The Associated Press recap of Dallas at Carolina began like this:

> CHARLOTTE—Tony Romo waited four years to get his first NFL start. It looks like he'll have the job for some time . . . Romo rallied Dallas from a 14-point first-quarter deficit, throwing for 270 yards and a touchdown . . . to help the Cowboys beat Carolina 35-14 Sunday night. Dallas set a team record with 25 fourth-quarter points . . .

When Tom Brady made his first professional career start in Bledsoe's absence as an advance write-off, his underdog team won by 31 points. Romo's first professional career start, also in Bledsoe's absence, produced a win by 21 points for his underdog team. The Cowboys out-first-downed Carolina 27-16 and controlled the clock for 39 minutes, which didn't surprise anyone who had done their homework while all the distracted media watchers were incorrectly focused on the fantasy that was being sold cheap—that Dallas was in disarray. For a season-and-a-half, the Panthers had been averaging only 17 first downs per game!

You know how they advise overly excessive on-field celebrators to act like they've been there before? The same principle applies in NFL forecasting. Act like you've been there before. If you watch the NFL, you've seen it all happen before in some way, shape or form. Why not act like it?

The most appropriate part about the aftermath of this game: Dallas promptly lost and did not cover the spread in its next game; the Panthers—for whom the defeat against Dallas was a second straight loss—won and covered their next outing. The media would incorrectly label the zig-zagging of fortunes as "ironic." It is merely NFL reality. Last week's game was, is, and always will be last week's game. The next opponent creates different matchups and strategies, and a new set of circumstances.

• • •

ONLY ONE WEEK before the New York at Dallas game, Monday Night Football was the stage for a rookie Heisman Trophy winner to make his second career start at quarterback for the Arizona Cardinals against the visiting, unbeaten Chicago Bears. Matt Leinart had been the Heisman Trophy winner for the national champion University of Southern California Trojans in 2004, stayed for his senior collegiate season in 2005, and had his ego and his expectations driven up by his agent and the media that told him how great he was. The NFL general managers spoke volumes of truth about him when the media—and, therefore, the Straight-Up fans—had expected to be drafted number one overall; he instead "slipped" to be the tenth player chosen in the first round.

How can somebody "slip" when they're not doing the moving? The concept is beyond any rational thinker's realm. Saying that Leinart "slipped"—then not being challenged on it publicly—is a terrific example of how the sports media has numbed the public's mind. Events that have yet to happen, where the subject being referenced can exert no control, are instead accepted as absolutely inevitable. Then, when the individual NFL team personnel directors and financial decision-makers responsible for setting the wheels in motion don't follow the prematurely established projection made by the media, the media reports that the player has "slipped" on the draft board. Amazing, is it not?

On October 13, 2006, ESPN's then-Monday Night Football crew of Mike Tirico, Tony Kornheiser, and Joe Theismann snuggled themselves into Matt Leinart's jockstrap for a cozy evening of sweet nothings to support the network's promotional hype. The 5-0 Bears, the −10 favorite off two lopsided home wins aided by turnovers, had no extended game tendencies of Leinart available to study. Chicago also had a color-blind quarterback—Rex Grossman—who tended to give the ball to the other side if Chicago's defense didn't first acquire a few turnovers of their own. Grossman coughed it up in his own territory early. Leinart, via several series of short, quick passes and yards made after the catch by Cardinals' receivers—offensive sequences that any fourth-string NFL quarterback could have negotiated—was able to nervously navigate the Cardinals to a 20-0 halftime lead.

Kornheiser was attempting to sell these 21 minutes of routine, on-field effort as an incredible individual achievement by Leinart at the onset of what was sure to be a Hall of Fame career. In reality, the Bears' mistakes, the game-plan prepared by the Cardinals' coaches, and the on-field support provided by Leinart's teammates accounted for the score at that time.

Leinart's third-quarter fumble in the shadow of his own goalpost was returned for an easy touchdown by Chicago and helped spark a 24-point second-half surge by the Bears to win the game, 24-23. Leinart's passing numbers were 24 completions in 42 attempts, for 252 yards. The Yards Per Attempt of 6.0 is below average for an NFL quarterback. Still, those numbers were lauded as evidence that Leinart was an early bloomer.

Any viewer or bettor who allowed Kornheiser and crew to do their thinking for them would come away with the impression that Arizona was a better team with Leinart at quarterback than with the guy he replaced, Kurt Warner. For emphasis, the Cardinals had covered the spread in this game for the first time in six tries. But naturally, 12 quarters later, the overrated rookie's team had been out-scored 80-33 and was 0-3 ATS. Leinart's average Yards Per Attempt of 5.3 in those three games was 2.0 Yards Per Attempt fewer than Warner's. This kid was nothing more than a dink-and-dunker with a rag arm. Leinart and the Cardinals had lost to the Bears despite a +5 Turnover Ratio. Teams that benefit from such a sizable disparity in that in-game category almost always cover the spread. But losing the game outright despite such a favorable turnover margin is the sign of sickness within, temporarily masked. In this case, the sickness within was further masked by the false praise for the "story-line quarterback."

A broadcasting crew is not always there to educate and inform the viewer. They are there partly to deliver misinformation that creates a sizzle among the shallow masses called a viewing public—the people who grant credibility to mediocrity time and time again. During the New York at Dallas game, the same Monday Night crew stooped so low as to take stands on which player would have the largest media contingent around his locker after the game! NFL coverage is 85 percent garbage by design, delivered with an agenda attached. You have to sift through it all very carefully to actually learn something useful.

Your local sports-talk radio host can be an equally poor a source of direction. You have to remember that sports talk radio exists to create a buzz. Buzz creates more excited listeners. Sports talk radio reacts to events and it asks its listeners to react to its reactions. It is a giant, time-wasting distraction spilling over with opinions from hosts and callers with too much spare time on their hands, and not enough sense to spend it more wisely. Very few voices on sports talk radio are truly in the know. This creates a misinformed public—not a bad thing as long as you do not become part of that misinformed public. When you make a determined effort to dig deeper to challenge shallow knee-jerk reactions, you can leverage the over-hyped filler called NFL media coverage to your advantage.

"Not only do I think that the Jets win this game, but I think they win it big!" Those were the words of ESPN 1050 Radio's New York-market co-host on a Friday morning in December 2006, five days after his tippy-top favorite team had dismantled Green Bay 38-10 on the road the Sunday before. He was not employed as an NFL forecaster, yet he was routinely making forecasts in the nation's largest radio market. To make matters worse, any listener that had made a relatively smooth transition into adulthood would have realized that this was the kind of guy who was probably still sleeping with the Jets-logo comforter his parents had bought him when he was in junior high. The fact that his radio station broadcast the Jets games shouldn't have made his "prognosis" any more believable.

"Winning in Lambeau!" was the host's criteria for proclaiming the Jets as having "lock" potential as a −5 home favorite vs. Buffalo that weekend. Hey, it might have been good criteria had the Packers themselves been winning in their historic—and therefore overrated—home confines. But they hadn't done it for three seasons! Through November that year, the Packers had only one home win in six tries. They were 3-5 SU on their home field in 2005, 4-4 SU in 2004. A lot of teams were waltzing in and out of Lambeau Field and winning!

But Jets-Boy—playing up the Bart Starr, Vince Lombardi image of the Packers that hadn't existed for 37 years, decided that he had witnessed greatness via a win in Lambeau that hadn't even impressed the other side's quarterback, Brett Favre. He had calmly told the media after the loss: "I don't know. I don't think the Jets are that much better than us. I'm not taking anything away from what they did. They made the plays, we didn't."

As Jets-Boy's homer forecast was beamed to hundreds of thousands of listeners, I regretted having set the *Sports Reporter* forecast for Buffalo at Jets to "Jets by 1," as a −3.5 favorite. Yes, we were leaning to Buffalo from the start. But sometimes, hearing the wrong forecast from a clown's mouth can shine the light on the soon-to-be opposite reality. It was suddenly very, very clear that the Jets would lay an egg, as we hinted they were capable of doing. Final score: Buffalo, 31-13. Straight-Up Jets fans like the ESPN radio host call themselves "long suffering." What they don't realize, is that they are suffering from something more than rooting for that particular team. They suffer from Square-Itis.

"In NFL football," Minnesota Vikings' head coach Brad Childress once told an inquiring sportswriter, "the worst performances can be followed by the best performance."

With those words of wisdom from a real weekly participant in mind—always in mind—our *Sports Reporter* forecast for a season-finale Giants vs. Washington Redskins match-up projected in favor of the Giants, who had lost six of their last seven entering the game and were coming off the worst loss of them all, by 23 points at home vs. New Orleans. Our analysis noted that there was another team in this mix, and that anyone impressed with the injury-decimated Redskins' chances of playing spoiler should note that in removing themselves from playoff contention after only 11 games, the Redskins were 3-8 ATS. "These are the Redskins," our argument closed. "When a goal exists, chances are they won't hit it."

If you had taken every Straight-Up report and "preview" on the game at face value, you would have concluded that the Giants should not have made the effort to show up. Yet, for a road game off a short week against an opponent they were favored to beat by 4.5 points on their home field in September, the betting line opened New York, –2. They were favored to win the game, which should have told the ridiculing finger-pointers something right there. All the negativity surrounding the team helped move the line to a close of Giants, –1. We placed the Giants to win by 4, released them as a small play to game-day customers on Saturday. The Giants won by 6. In their prior loss, the New York offense had not logged an offensive snap in the opponent's territory. Yet the very same group of personnel scored 34 points vs. the Redskins just six days later. Straight-Up Men were surprised. ATS Men were not, because it's not like a similar week-to-week, bad-to-good team performance contrast hadn't happened before on almost every weekend of every football season in history.

The only reason that anyone should listen to sports talk on the radio is to challenge every piece of content on it to learn what kind of junk and misinformation he should distance himself from while the general public dumbs itself down by buying into the emptiness of it all.

To be in position to win vs. the spread, it is very important to rise above the inherent coverage style of newspapers, radio, and television. Their take is for squares. If information from a media source taken literally at face value is the foundation for an NFL bettor's knowledge and decision-making process, that player is doomed to lose against the spread in the long run. If someone with a sharp forecasting foundation gets caught in a weak moment and runs with the masses, their time and efforts to avoid such a fate can be spoiled.

6

Challenging the Football Handicapping Media

THE OVERALL SOPHISTICATION of packaged-and-sold football forecasting content is about 25 years behind the times. For a very long time, the source considered to be the nation's leading authority on football "handicapping" was more like a culprit keeping the wagering masses stuck at amateur level.

In 1957, the Gold Sheet was founded. As far as anyone knows, that weekly was the first, continuously-published, national periodical dedicated to "handicapping" team sporting events. The Gold Sheet became revered for its supposedly enlightening "technical" information that spawned many imitators. Technical handicapping information is plainly and simply the point-spread record of a team in a given category, over a certain period of time. For instance, "New Orleans Saints, 7-2 ATS in last nine games as underdogs." The period of time represented within an ATS Record can be three weeks, eight weeks, one season, two seasons, five seasons, 10 seasons . . . whatever the publisher of that record wants it to be. The ATS record is researched and presented to create the strongest possible impact upon the reader. An ATS record is a back-fit grouping of results packaged into a presumably useful piece of data for the sole purpose of appearing fascinating and helpful.

Point-spread wagering was still in its infancy when the Gold Sheet publication debuted. Branded, packaged information to bet by was rare. Because football forecasting data was and continues to be so scarce, the "ATS record" became popular as a perceived "handicapping tool." Readers who were introduced to the Gold Sheet were immediately hooked to have their hands on anything that was catering to their interest in continuous football betting action. Imagining that if only they had discovered the Gold Sheet sooner, they could have been five games of profit ahead on something as simple as the notion of "Saints as underdogs" was powerful stuff that gained instant validation the first time it connected with a winning wager. They looked forward to more incredible "nuggets" of information, and the Gold Sheet was only too happy to provide them. The diminutive but fact-jammed newsletter had an enormous impact on the handicapping and sports betting processes despite having type too small to read comfortably, written forecasts too short to be seriously meaningful, and statistical facts presented with no study on how frequently anybody could expect that stat to lead them to a winner. It was a paradox, but "7-2 ATS as underdogs," or "2-7 ATS as favorites" stimulated people to bet on or against teams.

When the Gold Sheet's founder passed away in 2003, it was reported that his best friends in Las Vegas attempted to secure him a proclamation from the city. Why the city and its sports books did not follow through on the idea and go it one better with a statue is a mystery because for decades, by virtue of making this kind of information available and accessible, his product fostered a huge community of euphoric wagering squares. He and his eventual imitators were gurus who empowered readers to part with their money based on statistics that had little to no connection with the realities of the upcoming situations they would be wagering into.

"Expectations, anticipations, and hopes quicken the imagination, enliven the curiosity, increase the appetite and desires, and energize the action of all of us," wrote Dr. Maurice Green in the *Journal of the American Academy of Psychoanalysis and Dynamic Psychiatry*. "However, unrealistic and exaggerated expectations and anticipations lead to false hopes that pave the way for bitter disappointment, desperate frustrations and tragic despair."

That, in a nutshell, is "7-2 ATS as underdogs," which is what New Orleans was in 2006. For the first game of the next season, played on the featured Thursday night in front of a nationally televised audience to kick off the 2007 season, New Orleans was the +7 underdog at Indianapolis. They lost, 41-10.

Since there are only two sides in a game, the eventual result vs. the spread has a very reasonable chance to fall in line with the ATS record being presented. Also, since there are only two sides in a game, the eventual result vs. the spread has a very good chance to contradict the ATS record being presented. It's a win-lose-win-win-lose-lose-lose-win-win-lose kind of thing, similar to a cycle of junk food consumption. Addictive sweets can make people feel good, and they won't kill you in the short term. But they cause long-term problems, first and foremost being that anyone who eats them regularly is demonstrating an alarming lack of self-awareness and proving themselves to be ignorant in matters regarding the health of their own body. Just as your body slowly but surely breaks down from Coca-Cola intake, your mind and your wallet can break down by pouring heavily weighted football ATS records into them.

In a book entitled *Winning in the Futures Market*, author George Angell wrote that from 85 to 90 percent of all futures traders have been known to end up on the minus side over the long haul. "These percentages," he qualified, "should not sound as discouraging as they seem. Many traders, despite their protestations to the contrary, are not serious about making money in the market. Rather, they enjoy the excitement of buying and selling, watching price ticks in the boardroom, and the risk-taking involved in trading commodities. Some of these traders are inveterate gamblers . . ." There you go. Inveterate gamblers lack a serious foundation or process.

Unconsciously feeding their need for excitement and suspense—no matter how much it loses—is a pathological condition among the wagering customers catered to by many sports information outlets. If they had the ability to take a step back and analyze it, they'd be like most sane people who drop theories or beliefs when the evidence repeatedly fails to support it, like the fallout from these pearls of wisdom from Week 8 of NFL 2005:

Washington at New York Giants—Redskins 10-4 ATS as road underdog since 2003 season and 20-9 ATS in the role since 2000: Loser.

Green Bay at Cincinnati Bengals—5-0 SU, 3-1-1 ATS vs. NFC opponents under Marvin Lewis: Loser.

Philadelphia at Denver—Eagles 21-8 ATS as road underdog since 1999. Loser.

Buffalo at New England—Bills 4-9 ATS as an AFC East road underdog since 2000. Loser.

No sports information service has ever recorded results for these stale pretzel nuggets they toss at their customers, and few believers of this method among the betting public will be deterred. It's similar to astrology. One incorrect prediction after another will not sway horoscope buffs from their belief in the stars as a valid science. They might admit to some errors and slight miscalculations, but to them, the Zodiac signs and the system make perfect sense!

I tell any prospective *Sports Reporter* staff member that if they want to work for me, they'd better not be planning on wasting their time, my time, and readers' time researching ATS records. Before I accept anybody's take on any game, I need to know that the perspective includes an attempt at researching and understanding what is really going with the teams at the present time. I am not interested in learning that a team is 4-0 ATS in its last four games. I want to hear about a plan to capitalize on that team when that eventual fact is still in the womb! Get on that team at 0-0. Don't start telling people that Philadelphia is on a 4-0 ATS run after they have covered four straight games. That ship might have already sailed!

"Think about it," says an online forum host named Tommy. "If all you had to do was check over some simple mirroring of the bygone days to discover the outcomes of future games, everyone would be winning and sports books would be out of business. Using only trend statistics and ATS records is a dart throw over time." Sports books love volume dart throws, because they get 10 percent for every miss. Sports books are also becoming the worst abusers of disseminating ATS Records, using company-owned web sites disguised as sports information outlets to print ATS Records designed to lure bettors into sending them money that will help balance their action.

Since gambling is an activity with no requirements other than money in pocket, ATS Record angles can be a great carrot for a company to dangle as an apparently sophisticated tool to lead people into a wagering habit.

Sports books have picked up where the Gold Sheet began. Who breaks their neck in this industry to have ATS Records, trends and stats all over their web pages for easy retrieval? You guessed it, sports books. If they were so accurate, do you think for one minute they would make it easy for you to have that kind of information? Not on your life.

· · ·

BETTORS MUST SHOULDER some of the blame for the pervasive influence of ATS Records. They should have realized the shortcomings and the informational disconnect within them a long time ago. I have published several studies in *Sports Reporter* that disprove a very common tactic used by fake forecasters before a season starts: advising readers to play along the lines of a team's most recent three-season ATS record. In short, my studies have shown that if you group the best three-year performers in the categories of Home Underdogs, Road Underdogs, Home Favorites and Home Underdogs, and wager on them accordingly in every game the next season, you will lose money. By the same token, if you group the worst three-year performers in those four categories and wager against them accordingly in every game the next season, you will make a small profit.

ATS Records are made to be broken. Taking shortcuts to point-spread success will eventually leave you short of your goal. Anybody can make picks. Anybody. But there is a huge difference between a professional forecaster (some people might still call it a "handicapper"), and some guy making picks. Because anyone can make picks, and because anyone can write, it follows that anyone can call himself or herself a sports handicapper. There is no required course, no degree. No accepted discipline. In fact, anyone who puts "ATS records" on a page is often considered to be a sophisticated handicapper and that's just downright sad, because the reality is very much the opposite.

The saying, "A picture is worth a thousand words," has been around for centuries, but sports handicapping outlets haven't picked up on that. Otherwise, they'd have long ago enhanced their coverage by plotting a team's ATS course to give bettors a better sense of the degree and direction of a team's point-spread performance (see Figure 6-1).

Few companies in the sports info/point-spread picking business are in a position to look back on the fundamentals they preached and the suggested courses plotted before the season began—because they don't have any. They prepare by reading *The Sporting News* previews—Straight-Up nonsense written by Straight-Up writers. This is like taking Italian lessons before going on a vacation in France. Around October, they start telling you who is a "surprise" and who is a "disappointment," when they should have been expecting it all along. Many so-called "professional handicappers" are actually part of the public—looking backwards instead of ahead, because they didn't prepare by first looking backwards and attempting to ask questions about the past that might yield clues to the future.

A frequent rule of thumb that sports handicapping companies like to promote is: When in doubt, take the points. Sports books love that one, because it tells people that if they aren't sure, they should part with their money anyway. No way, Jose. When in doubt, you do not make a wager. You watch and you make an attempt to learn something.

•   •   •

SOME SO-CALLED PROFESSIONAL handicapping services owned by sports books are in full fraudulent form come NFL post-season time, when they attempt

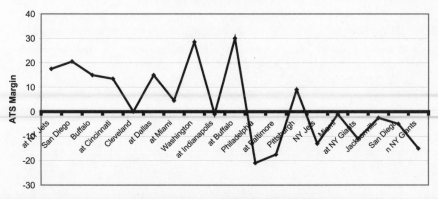

FIGURE 6-1 New England, 2007

to link past playoff results to the immediate future. With a smaller range of post-season games vs. regular season, it makes the ATS percentages less meaningful than they already were, if that is possible. This was an outstanding example from 2007, name withheld to protect the guilty, only out of kindness, for I generally have enough contempt to blatantly expose purveyors of stuff like this:

> *There are some basic trends that can help us when betting the NFL playoffs. Home teams are usually very strong straight up, winning at over 70 percent of the time. Against the spread they hold their own as well hitting at near 60 percent. Home teams that get the first round bye are also solid bets winning at over 62 percent of the time against the spread. Double-digit favorites are also a good bet in the NFL playoffs as they come in at over 65 percent of the time.*

In the 2007 NFL post-season that soon followed, home teams were 5-5 SU, 4-6 ATS, which represented 50 percent and 40 percent vs. the 70 percent and 60 percent cited as "basic trends that can help us." Help us what? Die sooner? Home teams with the first-round bye were 1-3 ATS, 25 percent vs. the 62 percent cited. Double-digit favorites were 1-3 ATS, 25 percent vs. the 65 percent cited.

• • •

"FREE PICKS" ARE a gimmick that online companies, whether they are owned by sports books or not, use to secure e-mail addresses. Give up your mailbox identity, and you gain access to junk like this from December 2007-copied verbatim—while opening yourself up to a wave of junk e-mail from the same source:

> *FREE PICK NFL—Miami vs. Buffalo: 3-Star on Miami Dolphins +7. This may be the Dolphins' best shot at ending their dreadful losing streak. Miami won't cash in their season due to not wanting the embarrassment of being an 0-16 team this year. Buffalo is a very beatable team that the Dolphins had on the ropes earlier this year. They held a 10-2 lead in the fourth quarter only to piss it away late. Miami can beat the Bills and we fully expect them to do so Sunday. The Bills are only scoring 15.3 points a game. Oddsmakers cannot justify this spread with those putrid offensive numbers. This game will be decided by a field goal as it comes down to the wire. The Dolphins are 6-1-1 ATS in their last 8 games following a double-digit loss at home.*

The Dolphins are 10-4-1 ATS in their last 15 games after allowing more than 30 points in their previous game. Bet Miami on the road.

Bet the warm-weather, injury-riddled, winless team from Florida that was scoring only 16.5 points per game in good weather, on a cold December day in Buffalo with sleet and freezing rain? Yeah, right. After Miami's 38-17 defeat, anyone who followed that particular free advice definitely got their money's worth!

7

Challenging the Oddsmakers and Bookmakers

BY MANY ACCOUNTS, Sonny Reizner was the most esteemed sports book manager in Las Vegas history. This could be the equivalent of saying that Satan is the most esteemed gatekeeper in Hell. He once said, "You don't even have to be especially smart to win at sports betting today."

Reizner's quote had a huge agenda behind it, and could not have been further from the long-term truth. But sports books are not in business to paint totally truthful pictures for their customers. A bookmaker is the ultimate volume dealer. The more people in action, the more money pumped into the pool, the better for the bookmaker. As soon as the money is in the bookmaker's hands, the bookmaker can move it around and position himself for his own best possible result regardless of whether any individual customer's wager wins or loses.

Sure, you could train a monkey to circle one side in a game, and the monkey's team could win. That monkey might then win again. Then, he might win again. Then, he might win again. All hail the monkey. In that respect, if Reizner's statement was rephrased to state, "You don't have to be especially smart to win a wager," it would have been true. After all, "Giants +3.5 at Cowboys" has only two possible outcomes. Either the Giants bettor gets paid, or the Cowboys bettor gets paid. A blind man with two pieces of paper in front of him-one labeled "Giants," the other labeled "Cowboys," shares the monkey's 50-50 chance of picking the eventual winner vs. the spread. But the monkey and the blind man also have a 50-50 chance of picking the loser. Multiply the blind man and the monkey by one million. Then, be aware that NFL sides purchased at $11 can only be redeemed when they cover the spread, and then for only $10. Now you see how the bookmaker—holding $11 from all comers and bound to return $10 only for each win—is well positioned to make a long-term profit.

If a book handles $500,000 in wagers, it earns some $25,000. If it handles $1,000,000 in wagers, it earns about $50,000. Because having a million dollars in hand is twice as good as having half a million dollars in hand, the sports bookmaker wants people to believe that they don't have to be especially smart to win at sports betting.

Ideally, the bookmaker would like the handle on each individual game to be balanced between the two sides. It can never work out perfectly for them, but they have ways of adjusting. One of them is by simple virtue of being forced to have a position on a game. If they are exposed in a game—say, 65 percent of the money on Dallas and 35 percent of the money on Philadelphia—the 35 percent side will win half the time in the long-term and the book will reap the benefits repeatedly, offsetting the losses when the 65 percent money team wins. Remember, the sports book is not vested in only one game. Sports books also play the shell game. When action is uneven in a given game, they have the right to call around to their competitors and find someone in the opposite boat—light on Dallas, heavy on Philly. Book A takes their Dallas-heavy balance and bets it with Book B, the Dallas-light team. It becomes a win-win for both and the game hasn't even kicked off yet, because each is moving closer to their desired goal of 10 percent with no risk on one side or the other.

Very contrary to Mr. Reizner's devil-may-care statement, you must be extremely smart to win at NFL betting. The man may have had many admirers among his peers and was probably very good at what he did. But his well-crafted, misleading sales pitch is an excellent example of the weasel-like manner by which a sports book operator will attempt to con people out of their money. With only 32 teams playing just 16 games per week and only 256 available games a year before playoffs, winning vs. the point-spread in the NFL is actually more difficult than winning in any other sport. Because of the low game frequency, the ranges involving all statistical averages that might be used to help predict the future are too small to be as meaningful as they might be in basketball, baseball, and hockey. The NBA opening day is usually on or about November 1, and by December 8, professional basketball in the U.S. will have completed more games than the NFL will conduct over the course of its entire season, which on December 8 is into its fourteenth out of seventeen regular season weekends. Percentages in any NFL category—individual or team, offensive or defensive, rushing or passing, game yardage or per carry/attempt, ATS records, you name it—are based on samples too small to be considered as serious trends. When the next season begins with 33 percent roster turnover and maturing or transitional systems, last season's statistics are subject to change that requires careful analysis and imprecise—or should I say non-guaranteed—projection. Expecting each season's small body of samples to carry over without qualifying them is a guaranteed way to lose. It takes a smart guy—a very smart guy—to develop the skill sets necessary to acquire and filter raw data and news information, have the patience for trial and error, the discipline to pass when unsure, and the confidence to make sound decisions and follow through on his convictions.

Sports books today are at the forefront pushing bad information onto the player. For example, take this misleading content on the Super Bowl page at BetUS.com leading into the 2008 Super Bowl XLII in Tempe, Arizona.:

When you first start betting on the NFL, the more football betting advice and knowledge you have, the more likely you are to fill your pockets with cash!

Not true. If most of your information and knowledge is bad, you are less likely to fill your pockets with cash.

In a promotional pitch for attracting wagers on the Super Bowl, BetUS.com stated the following:

Three points decide about 33 percent of all NFL games and 15 percent of all NFL wagers will be decided by seven points.

How many potential customers would be astute enough to challenge those statements and not just accept them at face value? Not many.

But my own 15-season records show a huge contrast from what that sports book stated as fact, and what I know to be true: First of all, the margin of three points has decided only 16.4 percent of all NFL games. Secondly, if you lump the difference of six-and-a-half points in with seven points just to be generous towards this particular bookmaker, then multiply that number times two to reflect people wagering on both sides of a single game, only 11.3 percent of all NFL wagers vs. the spread are decided by six-and-a-half or seven points.

The president of another online sports book once tried to dupe his would-be customers by advising them that 65 percent of NFL Week 1 games tend to go Over the total, despite the cold, hard facts to the contrary:

The sports book president said "65 percent Over." The actual results say 51 Over and 75 Under, which is "60 percent Under."

Either the sports book president was clueless as to common details of his own business, or he was lying in an effort to attract money onto the Over from bettors ignorant of the justifiable trend toward Unders. By virtue of having quoted a sports book operator, the online "sports information" media outlet that quoted him was certainly displaying its ignorance. I'd say that a sports book operator is the last person you'd want to ask for help on a bet, but that would be inaccurate. Comments made and information presented by anyone affiliated with a sports book should not factor at all in your pursuit of the actual truth. This is a source that should be completely ignored. By talking up Over, that sports book operator

NFL Week 1	O	U
2000	5	10
2001	5	10
2002	12	4
2003	7	9
2004	7	9
2005	6	10
2006	4	12
2007	5	11
Wk 1 Totals	51	75

FIGURE 7-1

could very well have been attempting to lure balancing Over action into his books to offset a larger share of the action being bet on Unders by the sharp players. By blanketing Unders across the board, the sharpies would reasonably expect to squeeze out anywhere from a small win (2003, 2004) to a windfall (2006, 2007).

During Week 12 of the 2007 NFL regular season, Robert Walker, sports book director at the MGM Mirage, managed to infiltrate the *New York Post*. On the Wednesday prior to the games, when the New England Patriots were 10-0 and about to face the Philadelphia Eagles on Monday Night Football, the *Post* enabled Walker to plant a bad seed in the public's mind. At the time, the Patriots had covered every game except for one, when they had been favored by –5 at Indianapolis and won by 4 points. New England had been winning by huge margins on balance, so large that at the time, their average game result was covering the spread by 14.3 points, on pace to smash the most recent 15-year NFL high of 10.6 set by the 1999 St. Louis Rams. Walker was quoted moaning about how the bettors had been loading up on New England every week, winning, and costing the sports books money. Naturally, the public was not privy to the books that would prove his claims of losing, and the *Post*'s writer was reporting as fact the word of a bookmaker—funny joke, ha-ha. "Every week," Walker moaned, "it's a six-figure giveaway on New England. It's like one free bet each week."

One free bet, my butt. This guy Walker knew exactly what was he was doing, and the *Post*'s writer did not. The newspaper writer from Straight-Up America obviously was not aware that it was a bookmaker who once said, "You want to take the guy to the cleaners one shirt at a time." Right after Walker's "free bet" advertisement hit the newsstands in the nation's largest media market, the suckers lined up for their "free money" on New England, just like the devil behind the desk had advised them to do. A line that had opened at New England –17.5 got driven all the way up to –25 on the "perfect" 10-SU, nearly perfect 9-1 ATS Patriots against the road warriors for all time, the proud and poised veteran Philadelphia Eagles. To which we at *Sports Reporter* reacted with a 4-Star release on Philadelphia, +25, an outcome that was rarely in doubt in a see-saw, 31-28 win where –25 favorite New England was actually trailing in the fourth quarter.

· · ·

THE PHRASE "BEAT THE BOOKMAKER" is a misnomer that creates the mistaken impression that an NFL bettor is doing battle with the sports book. The book-maker is not a mystical guru with secret knowledge. The bookmaker is just a lout who buys his lines from a linemaker, lines that are calculated using seventh-grade math to determine power ratings for each team. The best approach to take when you are playing the NFL is to put both of those guys out of the picture and just concern yourself with predicting the future. Nobody needs to be concerned with beating the bookmaker. The money that anyone plans to win from a wager was not really the bookmaker's cash. The bookmaker's money was invested in his business' overhead and assets, plus the cost of buying lines from an outside service. Winnings originally belonged to another bettor and the bookmaker was merely holding it. Nobody should aim to beat a mere middleman.

Anticipate what's about to happen in the games. Establish an objective to pre-dict the future. When you do, and you start hitting your goals, that important other thing—winning—will take care of itself. Las Vegas bookmakers love to inflate their importance and influence, and they have done a good job of furthering the mystique. They have done such a good job of it, that football forecasters with fair reputations actually believe the hype about them. Paul Zimmerman, a long-time NFL prediction writer for *Sports Illustrated*, author of seven books about the NFL, also known as Dr. Z., exposed his square side prior to Super Bowl XLII when he was interviewed during game week by a blogger who asked, "You called for a Giants' upset [eventually proven correct]. Are you still feeling good about it?"

"No," said Zimmerman without hesitation. "I'm not feeling good about it because the number opened at 12.5. It's too much. It's like Vegas is begging for Giants money. I don't like to be trapped by those people. They know more than anybody and the number hasn't come down. If it would have opened at about 7, and the idiots would have bet it up to about 8.5, I'd feel a lot better. But that's making me nervous . . . You've got to look at Vegas. The people who set the price aren't idiots." *Are we a little paranoid, Doc?*

Professional handicapping clowns with dubious reputations also like to refer-ence Vegas to make themselves sound like the wise guys they wannabe, never were, and never will be. To make matters worse, the Straight-Up media is sometimes there to frame what they say in front of the general public. The *New York Times* actually quoted a Long Island-based selection-service operator named Stu Feiner in a story about Super Bowl wagering in its February 3, 2007 edition. His side was 18-0 SU New England, –12 over New York. His reasoning? "Vegas doesn't give away money. They're using the point-spread to suck you in to take the Giants. Giants fans think they're team is going to win outright, so you throw in 11 points and it seems like a great pick. But the public is usually wrong, so if you want to be successful, you have to go against the public, against the grain."

Translation: "No idea what I'm talking about, but it sounds good to my clients who I can con into thinking that I know what Vegas is thinking, and that Vegas knows what the outcome will be."

The only thing that Vegas is thinking is how it can play its real role, which is to attempt to draw as much money as possible into their pools. The 10 percent juice is the gimmick that allows them to survive like a carnival owner who rigs the bottle-ring and basket-toss games.

A common mindset among some experienced, logical, sound NFL forecasters is to look for "bad lines" to attack. I do not share this mentality. This chapter is loaded with knocks on bookmakers and linemakers as overrated pieces of the puzzle. They are almost non-entities, really. Yet I also say that the linemaker and the bookmaker are perfect at what they do. They are so perfect, that they should be ignored as soon as the lines are published. There is no such thing as a bad line. How could there be a bad line?

Two teams each have a power rating, calculated by the linemaker based on prior results. The linemaker does seventh-grade math, with a sophisticated computer. Then he adds 3 points for the home team, another move a seventh-grader can make. The bookmaker acquires the numbers and either leaves them alone, or adjusts based on gut instinct. The line moves a little this way or that way or stays the same, based on the amount real-time money wagered on one side vs. the other, and the individual book's willingness to expose itself to risk if the two side amounts are not close to equal.

Fine. Dandy. The line is right. It is what it should be. It gets made in the same manner for every game, every time. The point-spread is what it is. It is out there. It is known. Even though it is possible for four different prices to be purchased on one team by thousands of bettors depending on where and when their bets are placed-for instance, Dallas Cowboys at –6.5, –7, –7.5, or 8-the line is always right.

However, the result is still to come. The result will be what it will be. The result is destined to land from 0 to 45 points away from the already established spread. Why fight the spread or the people and factors that created it—including yourself, since your wager will represent a tiny fraction of the overall percentage? Your mission, should you decide to accept it, is to try to pick results that land the farthest distance from the spread on the winning side of it (to give yourself an in-game margin of error). Just like a bookmaker is only concerned with volume, you should only be concerned with picking sides that cover by at least two scores. It's not easy, but you can facilitate the task by refusing to waste time and energy worrying about influence that linemakers and sports books might have on a result, because they have none.

As far as pure football knowledge is concerned, Mickey Charles, president of the Sports Network wire service, is very much on target when he says, "The odds maker knows precious little more than you do." Incredibly, 60 years into NFL betting, Straight-Up Men and inexperienced ATS Men still marvel at how the odds makers really seem to know who is going to win, and by how much. The odds makers and sports books put on a good face for the public when a –7 or –7.5 favorite wins by 8 points. The non-sophisticates say, "Boy, they made the right line," and the sports books nods in acknowledgment, as if to indicate their superiority over everyone else involved in the prediction game.

No way, Jose. Sorry. It's a façade. If the –7 or –7.5 favorite had won by 20 points, the line of –7 or –7.5 still would have been right. Here is the irony behind the erroneous premise that NFL results landing on the point-spread are evidence of incredible inside knowledge by the linemaker and sports book: A 27-20 victory by a –7 favorite is a tie vs. the spread. In a tie vs. the spread, the bet is refunded to both sides! Nobody is in business to give money back. The last thing the sports book wants to do is issue refunds on all the money in a game pool! That money is already in their clutches! They sure as hell are not going to feel as smart as people think they are when they are handing money back on games "they" said would end that way!

Remember something. The games came first, and were resulting the way they did, are now, and always will, before anyone started making lines on them. Bookmakers are so sinister that they fabricated a score calibration that doesn't exist in the NFL as another edge in their bag of tricks—the half-point! When the guy who invented the half-point died, Beelzebub himself probably made sure to be at the fiery gates of hell to wish him well in the afterlife!

When the final margin of a game lands on or near the spread, it's not because the linemaker knew it would, or because the linemaker made a 'solid line.' The result lands near the spread as a function of the line having been calculated and created in the most efficient manner possible! By the simple virtue of the games merely taking place, some will land on or very close to the spread! Just like when you leave the house to go the train, your arrival time at the platform will land within a certain number of minutes from the arrival time of the train, depending on when you leave the house, and how much traffic you encounter on the way to the train! If you leave early and breeze through the streets, there will be a large, favorable gap between your arrival time at the platform and the train's arrival. If you leave late and encounter much traffic, there will be a small, stressful gap, or you will be late. But one thing is for damn sure—nobody is making on a line on your commute to the train.

If there were no lines made on NFL games, they would still have a final margin (assuming the league was still able to exist minus the wagering option to make it interesting). Why do oddsmakers and sports books get credit for making a "good line" when the final margin happens to be in the same neighborhood as their point-spread? Because they have been able to con the public that they are smarter than they really are, with much assistance from the Straight-Up and ATS Media. But as far as actual football knowledge goes, the sports book is a blind squirrel in Nut Gathering 101 class with a seeing-eye dog performing his math homework. For the 15 seasons from 1993 to 2007, the median margin of the final score vs. the point-spread (ATS Margin) of all NFL games was 8.5 points. (For purposes of comparison, the median ATS Margin is 10 points in college football, 7.5 in the NBA , 6.5 in college basketball.)

Another misconception that, strangely enough, is pervasive among experienced bettors is that NFL point-spreads are "softer" and more exploitable at the beginning of the season than they are later on. Regular wagerers have somehow been conned into believing that lines are out of whack early, then get "tighter" late in the season after the linemaker has "had a chance to watch the teams play and evaluate them." *This is so untrue, Mr. Magoo.*

Over the course of the same 15 seasons, 26.7 percent of Week 1-3 games landed from 0-4 points from the spread while 26.0 percent of Week 12-14 results fell within the same 0-4 range. Extending the decisive margin vs. the spread to 0-7 points, you find 40. percent of games in that range in Weeks 1-3, 41.3 percent of games in that range in Weeks 12-14. The differences are negligible.

The best way to describe a bookmaker is as a less attractive and more deceitful version of Vanna White, the woman who made a career of adjusting letters based on people's guesses on a nationally televised, nightly game of hangman called *Wheel of Fortune*. The bookmaker makes a career of adjusting numbers based on people's guesses on nationally televised football games, and is required to know as little about the NFL as Vanna White is required to know about Phrases, Places, and People, the subjects that comprise the game show's word puzzles. Bookmakers might as well be walking around in high heels, rhinestone-studded dresses, smiling the big smile, pointing seductively between the odds board and the player with long, elegant shiny red fingernails and whispering, "Come on, big guy, buy a vowel."

Part Two
The Practical

8

Change is Constant

*F*UTURE SHOCK WAS a book written by Alvin Toffler, a former writer for *Fortune* magazine who became known as the world's most famous futurologist. Toffler, who coined the phrase, "information overload," once said, "In describing today's accelerating changes, the media fire blips of unrelated information at us. Popular forecasters present lists of unrelated trends, without any model to show us their interconnections or the forces likely to reverse them. As a result, change itself comes to be seen as anarchic, even lunatic."

Anyone who follows sports is familiar with the "First to Worst" phenomenon in the Straight-Up sense—when a first-place team finishes last the following season. Have you ever noticed that despite the very commonplace nature of this occurrence, the majority of people living in Straight-Up America, as well as too many ATS World residents, seem to be surprised when it happens?

Straight-Up Man has an excuse for thinking this way. After-the-fact reaction to the surprises and "unpredictability" of the NFL is what he is all about. Straight-Up Man eats a steady diet of "Most Disappointing" and "Most Surprising" articles churned out in late September and October to fill space in print and online.

But when ATS Man falls into the same trap, eating the filler and getting fat, happy, and out of shape, there are no excuses.

We've already covered the fact that despite 33 percent average roster turnover per team from season to season, the average number of points scored and allowed per NFL team doesn't rise and fall in proportion to the roster turnover. Players are, essentially, mere numbers on a uniform. Dynamic difference-making players are the exception that proves the rule. When the best players at each position are removed from the picture, does anyone really think that within the remaining group that there is actually a tangible, calibrated difference between, for instance, the NFL's best and worst remaining wide receivers in a group of about 100? That's a rhetorical question, because the answer is roster turnover. Squares believe it, bettors do not. The media is full of stories that purportedly "rank" the "best" players, as if the people doing the ranking had any idea what they were doing. What they are actually doing is filling space while seriously deluding their readers, viewers, and listeners. They also seriously delude themselves, as the New York Jets and Detroit Lions deluded themselves when they drafted wide receivers named Keyshawn Johnson and Calvin Johnson with the first picks in the 1996 and 2006 drafts. The wide receiver ranked 100th by statistics or, worse, by a poll, could easily outperform the wide receiver ranked at the top of the list if they were playing on opposite sides in the same game.

Once again, the point must be made: Parity rules in the NFL. Nearly all the governing factors that take place before each season begins are designed to draw the teams as close together as possible. Those rules are the constants that liberally exert degrees of control over teams' capabilities. But what cannot be controlled is the cumulative random effect of the 33,000 mass collisions that occur after the season's opening kickoff. The most extreme of these effects—injuries and turnovers—are rarely repeated with the same frequency from one season to the next. The teams with the least injuries tend to stay in sync by playing more starters more frequently, using reserves as reserves when needed, not as starters out of emergency necessity. Therefore, they are in position to make fewer turnovers and acquire more than teams with greater degrees of injury issues.

In the 2006 regular season, the Baltimore Ravens were 13-3 SU, 10-6 ATS. They stayed relatively injury-free throughout. The Ravens accumulated the league's best turnover ratio: +17. To the untrained eye, it seemed like a terrific number, and it was. Key word: "Was." Baltimore's Turnover Ratio from the 2005 season had been −10, making the year-prior difference of +27 the NFL's greatest positive Turnover Margin change. From that high level, it positioned the 2007 Baltimore Ravens to take the NFL's greatest fall. There was nowhere to go but down. It didn't guarantee that Baltimore would take a major tumble—there are no guarantees in life or football—but it made them a very strong qualifier for an off-the-charts plummet. Why was this dire fate very predictable before the Ravens would even play a game in 2007?

In the 2007 Baltimore Ravens media guide, text on pages featuring head coach Brian Billick and defensive coordinator Rex Ryan gave each man credit for +17 Turnover Ratio, "good for best mark in the NFL." During pre-season, John Clayton of ESPN wrote the Straight-Up and narrow take in a favorable "preview" of the Ravens: "Coach Brian Billick and the Ravens added QB Steve McNair, and the Ravens' scoring average went from 16.6 to 22.1 points per game . . ."

In our *Sports Reporter Zone Blitz*, I tried to be as doom and gloom as possible regarding the Ravens and said that a rosy outlook, was typical oversight by regular, tired, and dull sportswriters who continually miss the real point in projecting because they are too lazy to dig for the underlying causes for what lies ahead. "The 2006 Ravens rushed for fewer yards per carry, improved their completion

Prior Year	#1 TO Change Team	TO Ratio Change	ATS	Next Year	TO Ratio	TO Ratio Change	ATS
2004	Buffalo	+26	11-5	2005	+4	–6	6-10
2005	Denver	+29	11-5	2006	0	–27	5-11
2006	Baltimore	+27	10-6	2007	–17	–34	3-13

FIGURE 8-1

percentage only minimally, and realized the bulk of their scoring increase by virtue of a Yards Per Point Ratio that was reduced from 18.8 in 2005, to 14.7. In a Week 2 game alone, Baltimore's offense netted just 56 yards on 3 drives, yet scored 3 times . . . McNair gets no younger, and his QB Rating of 82.5 last season was one point under his career average . . . Also, the Ravens lost only 5 fumbles last season. While McGahee might break some longer runs than former jailbird Jamal Lewis did, does the prospect of two new players in the backfield create more volatility in care of the ball? TO Margin Change of +27 is a problem. The last two teams who entered an NFL season after making the biggest TO Margin jump lost a lot of money vs. the spread when it was over."

You can see in the Figure 8-1 how horrible the 2007 Baltimore Ravens performed against the spread: worse than the money-losing Buffalo and Denver teams that had been perched at the highest level of Turnover Change in each of the two seasons before them.

Less than four days after the 2007 regular season ended, this headline appeared: *"Ravens go for total change as Billick, staff fired."*

They lost their freaking jobs! Over what? Injuries and luck! The *Baltimore Herald Examiner* reported the following: "The Ravens went from 13-3 in 2006 to 5-11 in 2007, in part because of injuries to Steve McNair, Kyle Boller, Todd Heap, Ray Lewis, Trevor Pryce, Chris McAlister, Samari Rolle, Jonathan Ogden, and even kick returner B.J. Sams. The Ravens began limping to the training room during the very first game, when McNair pulled his groin on the second play against Cincinnati and [tackle Jonathan] Ogden aggravated his hyperextended big toe. Fifteen games later, Baltimore was starting third-string quarterback Troy Smith and Ogden was contemplating retirement . . . The Ravens started 4-2, then lost a franchise-record nine in a row. Much of the blame was heaped upon a turnover-plagued offense that showed little imagination."

Should anyone have been shocked that the Ravens went from penthouse to outhouse in the course of a mere 16 games? Hell no! The precedent had been set. A +27 TO Margin Change, with their ordinary offensive personnel and aging defense, placed them on the threshold of extinction, not a pedestal to contend for the Super Bowl or continue to cover point-spreads! I noted how in 2006, Baltimore had lost only 5 fumbles. In 2007, they coughed it up 26 times, six more than the next biggest bunch of bobble-heads, the Oakland Raiders!

When the 2005 Buffalo Bills were coming off a +10 TO Ratio season of 2004, things were looking up. Or so they thought. The Bills had a winning record in 2004, and were also 11-5 ATS. But the +26 TO Ratio Change from 2003 to '04 had inflated their power rating to a point where it was almost mandated that in order to once again be a Straight-Up and ATS success, an aberrational achievement had to be improved upon. Since the second-season head coach Mike Mularkey was changing quarterbacks from 12-year NFL veteran Drew Bledsoe to rookie J.P. Losman, it was almost laughable to think that there was anywhere for Buffalo to go but down.

And, what happened to the coaching staff at the end of 2005? They lost their freaking jobs!

Ridiculously high Turnover Margins or Turnover Margin Changes create euphoria and unrealistic expectations. Any formal logical system depends on evidence to establishing truth. We need facts to recognize truth. Yet the fact that the highest Turnover Margins and Turnover Margin Changes cannot be sustained by certain groups of players and coaches continues to go unrecognized. Your evidence to that effect is in Table 8.1. As Turnover Margins make their inevitable regression from the unsustainable level set the prior season, everyone on the team is put into the lose-lose position of having to work harder than they are capable of working. Eventually, they just break down from the effort.

Drastic net turnover changes create freaky results that are most likely to be one-year wonders destined to head the opposite way. But these levels, and their effects, are not officially recorded or reported. They require digging and creative assembly on your part. Losing turnovers thwarts the gaining of yards. Acquiring turnovers overcomes the yielding of yards. Just as the teams with aberrational positive TO Ratio changes from one season can easily regress the next, teams with aberrational negative TO Ratio changes are eligible to rise and be profitable the very next season. The 2006 NFL season saw phenomenal rebound performances by the teams that had experienced the four greatest negative TO Margin Changes from 2004 to 2005:

A nice Turnover Ratio of +7 posted by the 2004 New Orleans Saints was a modest gain of +8 from the team's −1 TO Ratio of 2003, so the net change did not raise any red flags—certainly not with Buffalo up there with the net change of +26. But Hurricane Katrina devastated the Saints' home city just prior to the start of the 2005 regular season, forcing the Saints to play 16 road games. Completely

2005 ATS	2006	'04–'05 TO Ratio Change	'05–06 TO Ratio Change	2006 ATS
5-10-1	New Orleans	−31	+20	10-6
9-6-1	San Diego	−23	+21	9-7
6-10	NY Jets	−23	+6	11-5
7-9	Baltimore	−21	+27	10-6

FIGURE 8-2

removed from their accustomed routine and playing with the ultimate of distractions, the Saints ultimately posted a dismal Turnover Ratio of −24.

The coaching staff lost their freaking jobs!

Heading into 2006, New Orleans' net change of −31 was at the opposite extreme end from Denver's +29. Just as the Broncos' high expectations would be unrealistic, so would continued low expectations be a false assumption for New Orleans. The Saints' bottom-rung position on the Net Turnover Change scale was telling everyone who knows the language that most of the bad statistics and records from 2005 could be excused, and subsequently improved upon. A new coaching regime had an available mess to clean, always a key trigger to pending sharp improvement.

None of the four teams had made the playoffs in 2005. All four qualified for the 2006 post-season and the Saints would eventually record the most "startling" results, going to within one game of the Super Bowl before being eliminated. A flat $100 on all four teams in the 2005 regular season would have netted a loss of −$1,150. In 2006, the same process would have yielded a net gain of +$1,470, just by targeting and then isolating four of 32 teams in the NFL.

Fumble Recovery Rates

When a live ball hits the ground and is loose and free in the NFL, statistics show that each team has about a 50 percent chance to recover it. When the Carolina Panthers recovered 76 percent of opposing fumbles in 2005, you could have said they were lucky. When the New Orleans Saints lost 82.6 percent of their fumbles that same season, you could have said they were unlucky. The season after these extremes were registered, Carolina went from 10-6 ATS to 6-9-1 ATS, and New Orleans went from 6-10 ATS to 10-6 ATS. While Carolina and New Orleans

Team	1993	1994	1995	1996	1997	1998	1999	2000	2001	2002	2003	2004	2005	2006	2007
Arizona	5.3	-2.1	-5.8	-1.2	-2.1	-3.1	-5.1	-8.6	1.3	-4.7	-7.4	1.6	-2.6	-1.2	0.7
Atlanta	-0.5	-2.6	1.9	-6.4	1.2	7.3	-4.1	-4.8	-3.1	3.8	-3.2	-1.6	-1.5	-3.2	-4.0
Baltimore				-2.1	1.6	-1.8	3.0	4.8	-2.1	-0.1	7.1	0.8	-1.0	7.0	-5.7
Buffalo	0.1	-2.9	-0.1	0.8	-4.6	3.9	3.1	-2.9	-4.9	-0.6	-2.0	6.2	-3.9	2.4	-0.9
Carolina			4.6	8.9	-3.6	-2.0	3.1	1.4	-3.6	0.6	-0.6	1.5	4.4	-4.8	-2.6
Chicago	2.7	-1.0	-0.6	0.4	-3.7	0.6	0.6	-4.6	8.5	-2.9	0.1	-1.4	3.0	4.2	-0.2
Cincinnati	0.6	-1.5	1.5	2.8	-1.6	-6.3	-5.5	-4.3	-1.4	-5.9	0.1	0.7	0.6	0.6	-1.7
Cleveland	0.9	6.8	-5.2				-3.1	-6.1	1.8	1.8	-1.8	-1.6	-0.5	-2.8	1.9
Dallas	0.4	1.3	-2.0	-3.7	-4.4	3.9	2.1	-1.2	0.3	-3.5	1.1	-5.8	-0.3	0.0	2.4
Denver	3.3	-2.9	1.1	3.4	4.2	2.3	0.1	2.8	-3.8	-0.4	2.3	0.3	4.8	-2.6	-5.6
Detroit	-1.3	1.9	5.0	-4.4	4.0	-1.9	1.6	1.5	-4.1	-3.6	-1.2	-1.4	-3.0	-1.9	-3.3
Green Bay	3.0	3.8	1.6	7.1	0.1	-1.4	-2.9	2.8	2.7	0.4	5.0	1.0	-0.9	-1.0	6.6
Houston										0.0	-1.1	1.4	-4.2	-0.3	1.9
Indianapolis	-6.0	2.1	0.6	-1.2	0.1	-3.0	2.1	2.2	-6.4	-0.9	3.3	5.3	3.4	-2.4	5.3
Jacksonville			-0.2	0.1	1.4	0.3	2.1	-0.7	0.6	0.6	-0.5	-0.1	3.0	4.1	5.8
Kansas City	-2.6	-1.4	5.6	-2.6	8.3	-3.3	3.6	-0.1	0.5	4.9	3.6	2.1	4.0	0.2	-3.0

Miami	-2.1	1.4	-1.3	-0.4	-0.3	1.7	-2.6	5.1	1.5	2.3	0.6	0.1	2.8	-1.2	-4.1
Minnesota	-1.3	0.1	0.9	-0.5	0.0	8.9	-1.4	-1.9	-5.1	-0.9	1.8	-3.0	-1.4	-2.0	3.6
New England	2.4	2.2	-4.1	3.1	1.2	-0.9	0.1	-2.1	8.2	0.4	5.6	4.3	-0.6	4.3	5.6
New Orleans	-5.3	0.0	0.3	-4.1	-0.7	2.0	-6.6	3.7	-6.1	0.3	1.1	-1.0	-5.8	5.9	-4.0
NY Giants	3.3	-0.9	0.6	1.1	4.3	0.2	-1.8	2.7	-3.4	1.9	-8.4	-0.4	4.3	-1.6	0.1
NY Jets	2.3	-3.0	-4.5	-4.4	4.2	7.4	1.9	0.1	0.8	1.9	0.4	1.8	-2.9	3.1	-0.3
Oakland	-2.5	-3.1	-2.6	2.1	-6.1	-2.1	3.9	7.3	-0.4	5.4	-4.9	-4.8	-3.1	-3.3	-2.0
Philadelphia	0.5	-1.7	-0.8	-0.5	-2.9	-5.3	1.7	5.5	4.5	5.9	3.1	1.8	-4.9	1.4	1.5
Pittsburgh	-0.8	2.9	0.9	1.6	1.1	-4.4	-0.7	4.9	6.1	-1.7	-2.4	5.8	3.9	-0.2	1.8
San Diego	0.6	3.6	-0.8	-3.1	-5.3	-1.6	0.3	-4.6	0.3	-1.3	-4.3	8.9	3.1	5.1	2.8
San Francisco	2.8	3.3	2.8	0.6	-0.6	0.1	-7.5	0.7	5.8	-3.1	2.4	-6.3	-2.2	-1.9	-3.5
Seattle	1.5	-0.7	2.9	-0.1	-1.1	2.7	-0.3	-2.3	-0.2	2.3	1.8	-3.8	6.3	-3.1	2.3
St. Louis	-6.0	0.5	-5.1	-2.1	0.3	-1.9	10.6	-4.4	4.5	-6.6	0.9	-6.2	-3.1	-0.3	-5.8
Tampa Bay	0.5	-1.6	-3.8	1.3	1.3	-0.3	0.4	3.6	0.6	4.9	-2.3	0.4	-0.2	-4.3	3.3
Tennessee	3.2	-4.7	4.7	1.3	2.4	1.6	0.6	3.0	-3.8	0.9	3.1	-5.6	-4.0	1.7	-0.8
Washington	-5.4	-0.3	1.4	2.6	1.4	-3.6	0.9	-3.6	0.7	-2.4	-2.9	-0.4	2.4	-2.2	2.1

FIGURE 8-3

Year	Team	W	L	T	$100 Flat Against	$100 Flat On
2007	Baltimore	3	13	0	$970	–$1,130
2007	New Orleans	6	10	0	$340	–$500
2006	Seattle	6	9	1	$240	–$390
2005	Buffalo	6	10	0	$340	–$500
2005	Indianapolis	9	6	1	–$390	$240
2005	Pittsburgh	9	7	0	–$290	$130
2005	San Diego	9	6	1	–$390	$240
2004	Baltimore	9	7	0	–$290	$130
2004	New England	11	3	2	–$910	$770
2003	Oakland	3	12	1	$870	–$1,020
2003	Philadelphia	11	5	0	–$710	$550
2002	Chicago	5	9	2	$350	–$490
2002	New England	6	10	0	$340	–$500
2002	Pittsburgh	5	9	2	$350	–$490
2002	San Francisco	4	10	2	$560	–$700
2001	Oakland	7	8	1	$30	–$180
2001	Philadelphia	10	5	1	–$600	$450
2000	St. Louis	6	9	1	$240	–$390
1999	Atlanta	6	10	0	$340	–$500
1999	Minnesota	4	10	2	$560	–$700
1999	NY Jets	8	6	2	–$280	$140
1998	Kansas City	7	9	0	$130	–$290
1997	Carolina	7	8	1	$30	–$180
1997	Green Bay	5	9	2	$350	–$490
1996	Kansas City	6	10	0	$340	–$500
1995	Cleveland	5	10	1	$450	–$600
1994	Arizona	8	8	0	–$80	–$80
15-yr.	**All Teams**	**181**	**228**	**23**	**$2,890**	**–$6,980**

FIGURE 8-4

were flip-flopping fortunes as their luck evened out, the 2006 Cleveland Browns were in the process of losing 17 of their own 23 fumbles, 74 percent. You could have said the Browns were unlucky that year. In the 2007 season that followed, the Browns went from 6-8-2 ATS to an NFL regular-season best 12-3-1 ATS. As a team's good or bad luck evens out, so does its point-spread results.

The 5.2 ATS Margin Threshold

If you want a team to target against during the course of a season, the 5.2 ATS Margin threshold has been a good indicator of pending doom. ATS Margin, as discussed in earlier chapters, is the team's average margin vs. the spread per game for the season. Given the effect of turnovers on outcomes, there is usually a proportional relationship between Turnover Ratios and ATS Margins. Teams with the highest turnover ratios tend to have the highest ATS Margins. As of the end of the 2007 NFL regular season, the overwhelming majority of the 27 NFL teams that played +5.2 points or better vs. the point-spread in a season then regressed significantly in ATS Margin territory the following season, often into the negative range.

However, it must be pointed out that nine of the 27 +5.2 ATS Margin teams (Figure 8-3) still would have netted a profit in the following season. Still, those nine teams represented only 33 percent of the entire group, and included franchises like New England, Indianapolis, and Philadelphia that were hard to argue against as having superior talent and coaching compared to other teams in the league at the time.

Heading into the 2007, two teams qualified as go-against targets via this "bounce down" criteria: Baltimore and New Orleans. (Yes, the same Baltimore and New Orleans teams cited earlier in this chapter as experiencing wild performance swings relating to season-to-season Turnover Margin changes. The public is constantly zigging when teams like this are zagging, zagging when the teams zig. It's like trying to corral a loose chicken!)

The Ravens and Saints combined to be 9-23 ATS in 2007.

A 6.4 percent Return on Investment over 14 years may not sound like much, but what is your bank's money market rate these days, hmm? Perhaps 5.5 percent at best? Also, a 6.4 percent Return on Investment going against "hot" teams from the year before sure as heck beats the −15.5 percent loss tagged to the suckers and squares who ride them!

You almost have to think of the NFL as a Bizarro World. Extremely positive results in certain categories are the bad seeds for extremely negative results the next. And vice versa.

9

Understanding Schedules

THE 2004 SAN Diego Chargers made six round trips from their remote outpost in Southern California across two or three time zones. In the first round of the playoffs, the Chargers hosted the New York Jets, who, although flying 3,000 miles to play the game, had taken only two round-trip flights of similar length, just one during the second half of the season, and who had a bye week after the first cross-country trip.

The Chargers were favored by a touchdown on their home field. The Jets won the game.

The 2005 San Diego Chargers also made six round trips across two or three time zones. The fifth such trip was on December 17, at Indianapolis, against a 13-0 SU Colts team. The Chargers won.

Then, the following two Sundays, they lost each game and were eliminated from the playoffs.

The 2006 San Diego Chargers made only four such trips round trips, aided by a once every four years non-conference rotation that landed on AFC West vs. NFC West. Spending fewer hours in the air and more on the ground corresponded to the franchise's best regular season ever: 14 wins, plus a winning record vs. the spread despite sudden and sustained favoritism with a power rating that had grown by two touchdowns over the course of the prior three seasons.

Then, despite a week off, San Diego lost in the first round on their home field to New England.

Head coach Marty Schottenheimer got the boot for failing to win a playoff game during his tenure. The Chargers had played their butts off on the road in this three-year span and were an NFL-best 10-1-1 ATS as road underdogs—just another example of how performances within the NFL competitive realm and the point-spread realm are two separate worlds. Being ultimate road warriors won them no awards and might have been a factor in creating late-season fatigue in advance of this hump they couldn't jump.

The 2007 San Diego Chargers got a new head coach. As part of the territory that comes with working for the San Diego Chargers, Norv Turner inherited a schedule that called for the team to make six regular-season road trips across at least two time zones. They were 0-4 SU and ATS following the first four, and with each defeat, Turner was lambasted by fans and media for being a bad hire, a guy for whom the Chargers were regressing compared to what they had accomplished under Schottenheimer. Never mind the decree that according to management, the Chargers had not accomplished anything under Schottenheimer. The public had spoken. The media had all but labeled him. Norv was a ninny.

But when the Chargers won their final two long trips, on back-to-back Sundays in December, it might have become apparent to some observers what had been going on all along. Despite a schedule as rigorous as ever, the 2007 Chargers had something left in the tank at crunch time. The season featured the fewest amount of carries per game by LaDainian Tomlinson, the NFL's leading rusher. By taking care of business on their home field (7-1 SU) and within their division (5-1 SU), Turner set things up so that Tomlinson's high-carry game of 26 (compared to three-year prior single-game high-carry counts of 37, 31, and 31) came in the final trip across two time zones, at Tennessee, a game that virtually clinched a post-season berth for San Diego and enabled them to reduce Tomlinson's load for the final three games, when he carried only 15, 19, and 16 times, all less than his average of 20.5 to that point in the season, an average that was already lower than his prior-season averages that spanned from 21.7 to 26 carries per game.

After Norv Turner and the 2007 San Diego Chargers had engineered a different path to the post-season than in recent years—losing more of the games that were played far, far away from home—they did something different to begin the post-season. Bingo! They won a game! Covered −10 points, too, despite trailing 6-0 at halftime. The team that San Diego fielded that day in early January had more healthy starters and back-ups on it compared to the 2004, 2005, and 2006 teams in December and January. Which is why, on the very next weekend, the Chargers were able to make a seventh trip across two or more time zones in 19 weeks as a "physical" team at its peak against a "finesse" opponent. They were the +9 underdog at Indianapolis, a rested home favorite. But since Norv had been doing his "resting" during the season, and we at *Sports Reporter* were dialed into his gig, we projected a BEST BET San Diego outright win at Indianapolis by the score of 27-24. The Chargers won the game 28-24, earning the right to make an eighth trip across two or more time zones in 20 weeks to play the AFC Championship Game at New England. San Diego was starting to come physically unglued from the strain of the schedule drain that no other NFL team was asked to endure. High-profile skill players within their offense were known to be at less than 100 percent physical condition. But Norv had left something in reserve. BEST BET, San Diego +12 at New England! Final score, New England wins by 9 as the Chargers had been managed all along to have enough strength to limp home contentiously!

Straight-Up Man begins each football season in May by checking off expected wins and losses for his favorite team after the NFL releases official team schedules. How cute. The typical Straight-Up Broncos fan would have expected 12-4 SU for 2007—splitting with Kansas City and San Diego like they always do, sweeping Oakland like they always do, winning all home games because of the Mile-High advantage, and winning all road games against teams with history inferior to Denver's. Joe Public Bronco would also have been very excited and proud that his team would be featured five times in a nationally televised night game.

By the same point in the year, the most progressive of ATS Men have already begun their preparation for the upcoming season with an analysis and review of the prior season, which they began in January or February after the dust settled. With a greater understanding of what happened last season and why, ATS Man then dissects the upcoming schedule under a magnifying glass, classifying and coding as many games as possible according to the situation. The games on an NFL schedule are almost like snowflakes. To the naked eye, they all look alike. But when you put them under your microscope, you begin to realize that not all games are created equal.

Being tied for seventh-hardest strength of schedule based on the won-loss records of opponents from the prior season was the least of Denver's issues here. If won-loss records from the prior season were a guarantee to be duplicated the next, then they might represent an important barometer. But they are not. That's why they play the games.

When you break down a schedule, you first want to isolate *division games*, which in this particular example (Figure 9-1) are *italicized*. Division games vs. division opponents are worth two in the standings in the race for first place. A wild card chase is avoided by winning the division. Ergo, their place is at the top of the priority list. NFL head coaches generally set a goal of going 12-4, achieved by winning all their home games and splitting on the road. Therefore, an NFL team's three division home games each season are the tippy-top, ultra-most important games an NFL team can play. For their first such game in 2007, the Broncos would face an Oakland team that it beat twice the year before (the Raiders had double-revenge, designated by "ORR" in the "Situation" column). Oakland would feature a new coaching staff and new ways of doing things. It would be a preparation nightmare, to be followed by a visit from a strong Jacksonville team, then a trip to Indianapolis to seek revenge against the Super Bowl champion Colts, followed by the second of the three division home games, against a San Diego team that had beaten Denver twice the year before (Denver had double-revenge, "RR").

Wk	Date	Site	Opponent	Time	Situation
1	9/9	at	Buffalo	1:00	-bc
2	9/16	h	Oakland	4:15	ORR
3	9/23	h	Jacksonville	4:05	
4	9/30	at	Indianapolis	4:15	R
5	10/7	h	San Diego	4:15	RR
6			Bye		
7	10/21	h	Pittsburgh	8:15	OR
8	10/29	h	Green Bay	8:30	
9	11/4	at	Detroit	1:00	ncr, -bc, -tr
10	11/11	at	Kansas City	1:00	-bc
11	11/19	h	Tennessee	8:30	
12	11/25	at	Chicago	1:00	ncr, -bc, -tr, 3r4
13	12/2	at	Oakland	4:05	4r5
14	12/9	h	Kansas City	4:15	
15	12/13	at	Houston	8:15	-tr, 5r7
16	12/24	at	San Diego	8:00	6r8
17	12/30	h	Minnesota	4:15	−1 day

FIGURE 9-1 2007 Denver Broncos schedule

Once the Denver schedule was labeled this way, you began to see things that weren't otherwise noticeable. There were no breathers before the bye! The Broncos' post-bye slate would really jerk them around, with no continuity of kickoff time (five of eleven games at 8 p.m. or later) and six of eleven games across at least two time zones, for a total of eight two- or three time-zone trips for the season—half of the schedule! Staggering, because when Denver flies eastward for a game, they lose hours. Gaining hours on the way back is not an even trade-off. Four of the eight road games would begin at 11 a.m. Denver time (-bc), which is three hours earlier than the typical Sunday game begins when the Broncos play at home. With four kickoffs at the earliest extreme, two at the latest, and three other home night games kicking off at 6 or 6:30 p.m. their time, the opportunity to establish and maintain normal game-day routine would hardly ever exist for the Broncos.

On top of all this, there were destinations involving travel off a shorter-than-normal break between games, giving head coach Mike Shanahan and his assistants less time to prepare for those affairs (-tr). For those games, the opponent would enjoy an advantage with the normal break between games (at Detroit, at

Chicago), or by being home for the second straight game (at Houston). Although non-conference road games—like Denver's at Detroit and at Chicago—can be the least important on a team's schedule (they are not accountable for tiebreakers until way down the tiebreaker line), they become as important as any other game when a team's record gives them no margin for error as far as the playoff chase is concerned. For instance, a non-conference road game for a team with a 7-0 record is a lot less important than a non-conference road game for a 3-4 team that might have already played and lost three home games, which was the existing scenario for Denver prior to facing Detroit while at a disadvantage. And, at 5-5, the non-conference game at Chicago also became important, yet the Broncos were heading into it with the same short-week disadvantage.

Before the 2007 season began, "coloring the schedule" made something else stand out against Denver's ultimate ability to cope with it: very unusual, almost unprecedented for their placement and succession, stretches of four road games in five weeks (4r5), five road games in seven weeks (5r7), and six road games in eight weeks (6r8). All would take place after the bye week. The negative cumulative effect could not be good. What good would an 11-day break for a Christmas Eve home game on Monday Night be when most of the prior 14 games were dealt as they had been? It was like sitting at a Texas Hold'em table and with hole cards of 3-4, and a community of 2, 7, 10, Queen, being dealt an ace on the river card. "Thanks, for nothing. Why am I in this game, anyway?" When the Broncos encountered early-season injuries to starters on the offensive line, and wide receiver, while playing with a starting quarterback who had yet to complete a full NFL season, and a defense that was being re-systemized by a new coordinator, every potential obstacle within that schedule became that much harder to hurdle.

Oh, there was more unseen stuff that was working against Denver, and it emphasizes the importance that head coaches place on preparation time. Because Denver and San Francisco were the last teams to begin 2007 exhibition play on an August Monday Night, they were the last teams to begin training camp, which equated to them having the least number of practice days leading up to the regular season. The 49ers' head coach Mike Nolan voiced his displeasure over the arrangement. "It's a disadvantage . . . We're not getting ready for the pre-season. We're getting ready for the [regular] season . . . to say you get less practices going into the season because your pre-season game is [last], that's kind of ridiculous. Let's all start at the same time." This disparity—in a league otherwise filled with parity—was such a big issue to Nolan that he informed the media that he and Shanahan were hoping to pass a rule change whereby every NFL team will begin training camp at the same time.

Forced to play the weak hand they were dealt before the season had officially begun, the Broncos didn't cover a game until the week after their bye. They never

Wk	Date	Site	Opponent	Time	Situation	PF	PA	SU	Line	ATS
1	9/9	at	Buffalo	1:00	-bc	15	14	W	-4	L
2	9/16	h	Oakland	4:15	ORR	23	20	W	-10.5	L
3	9/23	h	Jacksonville	4:05		14	23	L	-3.5	L
4	9/30	at	Indianapolis	4:15	R	20	38	L	+9.5	L
5	10/7	h	*San Diego*	4:15	RR	3	41	L	+1	L
6			Bye							
7	10/21	h	Pittsburgh	8:15	OR	31	28	W	+3.5	W
8	10/29	h	Green Bay	8:30		13	19	L	-3	L
9	11/4	at	Detroit	1:00	ncr, -bc, -tr	7	44	L	+3	L
10	11/11	at	*Kansas City*	1:00	-bc	27	11	W	+3.5	W
11	11/19	h	Tennessee	8:30		34	20	W	-2	W
12	11/25	at	Chicago	1:00	ncr, -bc, -tr, 3r4	34	37	L	+2.5	L
13	12/2	at	*Oakland*	4:05	*4r5*	20	34	L	-3.5	L
14	12/9	h	*Kansas City*	4:15		41	7	W	-8	W
15	12/13	at	Houston	8:15	-tr, 5r7	13	31	L	-1.5	L
16	12/24	at	*San Diego*	8:00	*6r8*	3	23	L	+8.5	L
17	12/30	h	Minnesota	4:15	-1 day	22	19	W	+2.5	W

FIGURE 9-2 2007 Denver Broncos final results

sustained any momentum after opening the season with two weak wins (losses vs. the spread) against teams with less talent and their share of other issues. They failed to cover all negative body-clock games (0-4 ATS), all road games off short weeks (0-3 ATS), all road games, period, with the exception of at Kansas City, a team in worse shape than Denver that was in the process of losing ten in a row to close their own season.

NFL players and coaches—more acutely tuned to the parity in their league than most observers—have a saying: "It's not who you play, it's when you play them." The phrase is different than the old standard, "On any given Sunday, any team can beat any other team," which was coined in the 1960s by the late Commissioner Pete Rozelle and was meant to draw interest in apparent mismatches for whatever upset chance there might be. "It's not who you play, but when you play them," means that there are many factors that can throw a team off, soften it up. Key injuries, to multiple skill players or to multiple players on a unit, such as the offensive line. A coach—with wins in the bank—decides to rest some players, or tries to win in an alternative manner to how they normally play. That could mean running more often than normal to protect the quarterback, and running more often with a backup running back to protect the number one running back. It could mean throwing more often than normal to give a shaky quarterback extra work, or playing a "vanilla" defense to protect a good scheme from being overexposed to future opponents. Teams often luck out and play against an opponent's "B" game, which was the case for the 2007 Broncos when Pittsburgh came to town and the Steelers deviated from their usual run overload. With three division games to follow for Pittsburgh, where the "A" game was more critical, they ran only 26 times, against what was the NFL's easiest defense to run against. The Steelers had been averaging 35 rushes per game prior to hitting Denver. But their running back Willie Parker was a key figure in their offense, it was a long season, and three AFC North foes were on deck. By running 33, 39, and 35 times in successive weeks against divisional foes, the Steelers swept Cincinnati, Baltimore and Cleveland. When that substantial and satisfying feat was complete, it placed Pittsburgh at 7-2, two games in front of second-place Cleveland, who they had already beaten twice to effectively make their lead three games against the Browns. The Steelers then traveled to the "lowly" 1-8 New York Jets, who were rested and ready off a bye week. Favored by –10, the Steelers became the NFL's largest outright losing favorite. Water off a duck, really, given where they were in the standings and what had been going on around them.

It's not who you play, it's when you play them.

In 2003, Jim Fassel, then head coach of the New York Giants, was perusing his schedule in August and looking ahead to December. "The toughest one is going to be playing in New Orleans in a Sunday night game, and then going back to Dallas the next week. It's always hard to get home at six in the morning on Monday, and then have to travel again the next week."

How right he was. However, by that point, the Giants were in the midst of an 0-8 SU, 0-8 ATS streak to end the season, a very injured team with only four wins. They lost 45-7 at New Orleans. At +12 the following Sunday in Dallas, they were as tempting as an NFL double-digit underdog can be in a rivalry game with revenge. Off the short turnaround, they lost, 19-3. But which side would win the next meeting, to be held in early October of the following season? The Giants, easily, turning the 16-point losing deficit around 180 degrees to win, 26-10, in the same place, Dallas.

It's not who you play, it's when you play them.

The better and more healthy a team is, the greater the chances they can overcome the inherent obstacles in a back-to-back, Sunday or Monday Night to Sunday situation. In 2007, both Green Bay and Indianapolis won and covered the back ends of such spots in the more difficult Monday to Sunday time crunch. Both games were played during the first half of the schedule. Both teams had byes before the back-to-backs began, which allowed the coaches to plan early and offset the upcoming time crunch. Both teams also played bad opponents—Kansas City and Carolina—whose respective points differentials were –6.8 and –5.0. Both the Colts and Packers eventually finished the regular season 13-3 SU, covering a total of 22 out of 32 games vs. the spread between them.

It's not who you play, it's when you play them. But sometimes, it is who you play that carries more weight. Kansas City and Carolina might have been able to make their prep edge work against less talented opponents. Indianapolis and Green Bay might have lost against opponents at or slightly below their own level.

It's not who you play, it's when you play them.

Do not get that concept confused with the square phrase, "Nobody wants to play that team right now," a popular overstatement used by broadcasters and other Straight-Up media types who latch onto a mediocre team that happens to be on a winning streak for one reason or another, as if that winning streak was destined to last forever. An unfortunate prediction on the Washington at Seattle wild card game of 2007 provided an excellent example of that common boner, where the predictor was so naïve that he used the all-important, "It's not who you play, it's when you play them," concept in the wrong context!

As the cliché goes, it's not who you play but when you play them. It's safe to say few teams want to play the Redskins right now. They may be the hottest team in football [4-0 winning streak], having pounded Dallas to secure their playoff spot. Mike Holmgren's Seahawks are a battle-tested group with loads of playoff experience. Bet on Cinderella this time. Prediction: Redskins 27, Seahawks 24.

It was pretty dangerous to assume that "few teams want to play the Redskins right now." First of all, professional teams do not think like that. They fear nobody. Secondly, the past was posted with plenty of teams that lost the next game after a four-game winning streak. Was Seattle not supposed to show up as a −3 favorite on their own home field out of fear of a four-game winning streak by the Redskins? I had already explained in *Sports Reporter* how Washington's four-game winning streak was a function of having caught opponents at the right time—not who Washington played, but when they played them!

- Dallas didn't care because the Cowboys had already clinched home field for as long as they would last in the playoffs.
- Minnesota didn't have a real quarterback.
- New York weather was very windy and tilted that game in their direction.
- The Chicago Bears really stink.

While the Redskins were using up all their energy and exposing themselves just to qualify for the playoffs on the final day of the regular season against an eased-up Dallas team, Seattle had played their last three regular-season games eased up after clinching the NFC West, knowing they would host a wild card game! While in eased-up mode, Seattle lost and did not cover the spread at Carolina and Atlanta in Weeks 15 and 17, losses that did not change the fact that the Seahawks would host the eventual six seed in a wild card game, which turned out to be Washington. Carolina and Atlanta (−9.2 points differential) were "bad" teams, to whom Seattle brought their B and C games, the better to have their A game ripe and ready for Washington, whom they led 13-0 at halftime.

If the Redskins were really such a fearsome bunch that nobody wanted to play, then their head coach Joe Gibbs would not have quit with one year remaining on his contract three days after Washington's eventual 35-14 loss at Seattle.

It's not who you play, but when you play them. Learn it. Live it. Love it.

10

Identifying Team Styles, Strengths, and Weaknesses

L EADING INTO THIS particular Week 14, 2007 game—Minnesota Vikings, –7.5 at San Francisco—the following piece of misinformation appeared that helped trigger a visualization on it: *"The Vikings are just 5-11 ATS as road favorites since 2001 . . ."*

Well, to once again emphasize the nonsense that is "ATS logging research," we were living in the year 2007, not 2001. Most people on Earth have different things going on in their life six years down the road, as do NFL teams. It would be the first time the Vikings would be favored on the road in this particular season, and only the second time they would be favored on the road since Brad Childress had become head coach in 2006. In his rookie season as the boss man, the Vikings had lost 9-3 on this same field, traveling into San Francisco as an injury-riddled team off a short week after New England had their way with them on Monday Night Football.

The Vikings struck me as a very strong opportunity—with the 5-11 ATS record as a bonus public diversion, a red herring. In being rebuilt by head coach Brad Childress, Minnesota was not constructed like the typical team whose home is indoors in a dome. They were big on the offensive line, and concentrated on running the ball, not passing. In Childress's first two seasons, their average game split on offense made this change:

Year	Run	Pass	Total
2007	160	175	335
2006	118	209	327

FIGURE 10-1 Minnesota Vikings

These Vikings were not the St. Louis Rams, New Orleans Saints, or Indianapolis Colts, home-dome teams with speedy receivers on artificial turf whose quarterbacks often threw for 300 yards per game and averaged 260-270 aerial yards per outing. The Vikings had less than ordinary receivers. Their #1 quarterback Tarvaris Jackson still hadn't played a full pro season and had a long way to go before he would ever be a consistently good playmaker. But the increase in rushing yards from the season prior—up to 160 rushing yards per game—at the expense of 34 fewer passing yards and 6 fewer passing attempts per game—was being triggered by a standout rookie running back, Adrian Peterson, supported by last season's capable first-string running back Chester Taylor, behind that large and good run-blocking offensive line.

To complement the offense's ability to gain rushing yards, the Vikings' defense was, for the second straight season, allowing an NFL-low rushing yards, fewer than 75 per game.

Clearly, Minnesota had an identity: "Run, Stop the Run." This was an inarguable fact, because they were rushing for the most yards and allowing the least. Until further notice—when their group of skill players either matured or restocked—Minnesota was playing the Run, Stop the Run card. If an opponent could trump it, so be it.

If there was an offense with less potential in its passing game than Minnesota's, it was San Francisco's. "As Gore goes, so goes the offense," was a very common refrain about this particular 49ers team, in reference to their #1 running back. The 49ers' home field was notorious for being long, soft grass, to nullify opposing wide-receiver speed and accent their own between-tackles running game. The playing surface was actually very conducive to the way the road team wanted to play! With San Francisco's offense averaging only 94 rushing yards per game, Gore hadn't been going anyplace special. Matched up against a defense proven to be elite in Stop the Run, the likelihood of Gore going anywhere but nowhere on this particular afternoon was pretty slim.

The 49ers offense had no real identity. At only 94 rushing yards per game, they were 10 yards below the NFL median while Minnesota was 52 yards above it. With only 163 passing yards per game—rock bottom in the NFL—the likelihood of San Francisco offsetting the rushing yard deficit with big pass plays was slim. The numbers said so. Boiling it all down further, San Francisco's offense was logging only 53 plays per game, to Minnesota's 58, and getting only 13 first downs per game, to Minnesota's 17. While the Vikings' offense had engineered a shift towards more productive running from 2006 to 2007, San Francisco was falling 30 percent short of its above-average NFL rushing yards per game from '06, and 9 percent short of its already sub-standard passing yards from the year before.

Meanwhile, nothing about the San Francisco defense indicated that it could make dynamic plays to change the complexion of the game. The Vikings'

Year	Run	Pass	Total
2007	94	163	257
2006	136	179	315

FIGURE 10-2 San Francisco 49ers

defense had more interceptions, more sacks, and San Francisco's quarterbacks were losing −23 yards per game to sacks, vs. Minnesota's −11.

When a team like Minnesota—with a clear and present identity and still alive for the playoffs, is facing a 3-9 SU team with a losing record and no identity, a mismatch is on tap because if just one thing goes wrong, the inferior team with no identity is placed in a position of digging a bigger hole for itself as the game progresses. The Vikings intercepted a pass on the second play from scrimmage and returned it for a touchdown. Minnesota led 10-0 at the end of the first quarter. Right then and there, Frank Gore was, for all intents and purposes, eliminated. He was there in body, but the spirit in which San Francisco wanted to employ him was killed. The Vikings didn't have a big rushing day—only 117 yards—but they kept the competitive rushing matchup within the established scale, allowing San Francisco only 73 rushing yards and forcing a bad passing team to come from behind. Naturally, the comeback didn't happen. Final score: Minnesota 27, San Francisco 7.

A stone-cold Run, Stop the Run team like the 2007 Minnesota Vikings will have problems against good quarterbacks on good passing teams. The 2007 Vikings were 0-4 SU and ATS against Green Bay and Brett Favre, Dallas and Tony Romo, and Philadelphia and Donovan McNabb. Those three opponents ranked in the top four of passing yards per game in the NFC in 2007, but also sported above-average rushing totals per game. Because those opponents were able to avoid Minnesota's defensive strength, they jumped out to leads that removed the effectiveness of Minnesota's offensive strength. Running teams with weak passing games are bad candidates to come from behind against a competent opposing defense, because they are better candidates to fall farther behind by making an egregious error when passing.

The numbers, rankings and yardage totals referenced in this example are not hard to find. They are readily available on the Internet at numerous web sites, like nfl.com, espn.com, sportsreporter.com. Does it involve some work to track down and isolate? Yes, it does. Anyone who doesn't want to do the work won't be a winner. Awareness of how many yards teams tend to gain and allow, and how they gain and allow them, and where those averages rank between the ceiling and the basement within the overall league, creates excellent visuals in your mind regarding the identity of an NFL team. Defense counts, too. Being aware of the frequency of runs and passes on both sides of the line of scrimmage adds another dimension to your awareness of a team's identity.

$$\bullet \quad \bullet \quad \bullet$$

WHY BE AWARE? Because the coaches are aware and are attempting to find ways to attack the other team's weakness, while avoiding being attacked by the other team's strength. In the NFL, there are very few instances of size, strength and speed mismatches. It's more about schemes and systems, and how they are utilized and exploited. The numbers tend to be a good, bottom-line measurement for how effectively teams are utilizing their assets, and to what degree their assets have been, and might continue to be, exploited. You don't need to be deeply schooled in the intricacies of schemes and systems when you have the numbers to help you evaluate their effectiveness. You already know simple math. Use it as a foundation. Then, as you gain more experience in evaluating matchups, you can learn more about the football-specific details as you go along. Eventually, when you eyeball a matchup, you'll be able to give reasonably confident answers to these demanding questions—with the point-spread in mind—like a quarterback who reads opposing defenses:

- Can they come back from a deficit?
- Can they control the clock and protect a lead?
- Are they a big-play team?
- Are they a small-play team?
- Do they have the hardest-to-overcome trait: quality balance?

I'm not a big proponent of rules of thumb, but when you ask the questions above about both teams in a matchup, and relatively clear answers materialize, it becomes easier to spot one of the following "play-ons":

- Strong running teams vs. soft run defenses.
- Strong passing teams vs. soft pass defenses.
- Strong run defenses vs. soft pass offense.
- Strong pass defenses vs. soft run offense.

Or, this particular play-against

- Soft defenses as favorites of a touchdown or more vs. moderate-to-good offense.

One particular overrated weakness in the NFL is a backup quarterback that has had the benefit of a week's practice. A previous chapter has already discussed how Tony Romo entered cold in the second half on national television to throw gasoline on the fire and go down in flames, then led the Cowboys to a convincing victory and point-spread cover in their next game following a week of practice with the first-string offense. There tends to be overreaction against backup quarterbacks. Going into the final Sunday of the 2007 NFL season, in games started that year by someone other than the starting quarterback on opening day, NFL teams were 61-55 ATS. The winning percentage vs. the spread of 53 percent actually represented the tiniest of net gains on a flat-wager basis. With only a sketchy "book" on the backup, preparation against him becomes more of a mystery. Or, the game can turn into a field-position battle with a truncated offensive game plan, and a "contain" plan on defense, the kind of game where the team rallies around the inexperienced quarterback, operating differently to prevent his shortcomings from being called into action against them.

The Philadelphia Eagles, during Andy Reid's tenure as head coach, displayed excellence at rallying around the backup when regular quarterback Donovan McNabb was injured while the rest of the team remained relatively healthy. They were 5-1 SU and ATS with Koy Detmer and Jay Feeley starting Weeks 12 through 17 in 2002, and 5-1 SU and ATS with Jeff Garcia and Feeley subbing for McNabb during the exact same regular season-ending stretch in 2006!

You have to remember that quarterbacks who manage to filter up from the 119-team college ranks into the 32-team NFL are better players on the whole than a typical backup college quarterback with the first letter of the school's name shaved into the back of his head. Given time to practice and a supporting survival plan, they're not just automatic sitting ducks back there.

Running back injuries are the second-most overrated absences. In 2006, the Minnesota Vikings scored a 10-point win as the +2.5 underdog at Detroit using their fourth-string running back Artose Pinner as the starter. Everybody in the world knew about the Vikings' injuries at the position, and everyone knew Pinner would start. He got 29 carries, 125 rushing yards and scored 3 touchdowns. If the team has a good offensive line and the opponent isn't one of the elite run-stoppers in the league, any old back can find a hole and run forward through it. The Super Bowl single-game rushing record is held by a guy named Timmy Smith of the Redskins, who gained 204 yards in Super Bowl XII vs. Denver. His career, for all intents and purposes, lasted 21 regular season games, 190 carries, 601 yards, 3.2 yards per carry, and 27.4 yards per game.

So many high hopes are held for some of college football's most high-profile yardage gainers who get drafted in the first round. Those hopes often evaporate when the linemen in front of them do not enjoy the physical edges their college teammates might have owned week-to-week, and when the running backs' own physical attributes cannot outrun or run over opposing defensive players as easily as they did in college. The net result of encountering more contact is that they break down earlier. Young, talented running backs who had yet to play two full seasons after being first-round draft picks—like Ronnie Brown of the Miami Dolphins and Cadillac Williams of the Tampa Bay Buccaneers—each missed the last 12 games of the 2007 season. Williams had already missed two games in his rookie season, and two more in his second season due to injuries in 2005 and 2006. Brown had also missed four games the prior two seasons. Moving forward in the NFL, the smartest teams will stockpile running backs with less of a gap in their overall abilities, and spread the salary room gained around other parts of the roster.

This will ensure that the most exploitable and difference-making injuries continue to be on the offensive and defensive lines. Because offensive and defensive linemen are not directly accountable for yardage statistics that broadcasters love to spew and fantasy league players love to chase, their contributions are underrated. The absence of a good defensive run stopper—if there isn't a capable backup—will create more first downs for the opposing offense and fewer chances with the ball for the offense whose defense cannot get off the field as readily. The absence of a good pass rusher—if there isn't a capable backup—reduces the number of potential bad down-and-distance situations for the opponent and makes it more difficult for even the best defensive backs and safeties to play their best possible pass coverage.

When the St. Louis Rams lost starting left offensive tackle Orlando Pace in the 2007 season-opener, a 1-6 ATS stretch immediately followed, all of them straight-up losses. The St. Louis starting quarterback, Marc Bulger, was sacked 10 times in the first three games of Pace's season-long absence, and hit so often that he was forced to miss the next two games. Bulger was one of the consistently highest-rated quarterbacks in the NFC. When he returned, he was promptly sacked seven times by Seattle in a 33-6 loss.

When the Philadelphia Eagles were forced to play one September '07 game without starting left offensive tackle William Thomas, the division rival New York Giants seized the opportunity and sacked Donovan McNabb 12 times, tying the record for most sacks in an NFL game. Philadelphia's top running back Brian Westbrook was also absent from that game, adding magnitude to the day's offensive problems that were mercilessly compounded by the presence of Philadelphia's former secondary coach as the new Giants' defensive coordinator. Needless to say, the domino effect resulted in a Giants win and cover. When someone who was once embedded with a team is suddenly the enemy, his former team's weaknesses are more readily exposed and capitalized upon, providing his new team has the personnel to exploit them. This dynamic phenomenon of coaching intimacy, which often flies under the public radar, is further explored in a later chapter.

11
Sniffing for Blowouts

I S THERE ANYTHING sillier than someone intending to make a large bet on a small to mid-sized underdog, say, +4 to +6 points, who doesn't think that underdog can win the game, but is serious with a notion that "I think they can keep it close?" An old buddy of mine from the *Daily Racing Form*, Mike Hammersly, used to say, "If I don't think an underdog can win the game, I'm not interested in it." Thinking an NFL underdog can just keep it close is being a little too cute, almost to the point of being naïve, almost to the point of getting oneself thrown out of the ATS Man club. If an underdog of that size is keeping it close but trailing on the scoreboard in the fourth quarter, it is in position to lose the game by more than a touchdown, which would lose vs. the point-spread.

Nail-biters are not to be embraced in advance. Whether they ultimately win or lose, games where the score margin straddles the point-spread late in the contest have the potential to cause gray hairs, baldness, tantrums, high blood pressure, paranoia, and a shortened life expectancy. Life can be stressful enough without close games vs. the spread to increase the *agita* factor.

Ultimately, a win is a win and the return is the same whether you cover by a half-point or three touchdowns. But the goal of every good NFL point-spread player should be to consistently win blowouts. The guy who calls a 6-point underdog a good bet because they should be able to keep the game close needs a major reality check. Your conclusion on any side in any game, like any poll, has a built-in margin for error. You must shoot for the easy cover—the one that seems to have the least chance of being busted by late weirdness. You want to win the games that are so lopsided at halftime that they needn't be monitored closely afterwards.

If you are not envisioning selections that can win comfortably vs. the spread, then you need to start. A good place to begin this visualization exercise is to be aware that plenty of comfortable margins are out there to be won. Like waves on

NFL Seasons	Games >14.5 vs. Spread
1993–2007	25.5%
2005–2007	27.3%

FIGURE 11-1

a beach, they just keep coming and will continue to keep coming as long as the NFL and sports books are in their mutually exclusive businesses.

In both sample spans—a three-year range of all 768 regular-season games, and a 15-year range of all 3,674 regular-season games—more than a quarter of NFL games have been decided by 15 points or more vs. the spread. That doesn't even count games that land from 9 to 14.5 points from the spread, margins which, like 15 points or more, also represent advantages or deficits of two scores. But the "9 to 14.5 range" is omitted for a reason: to demonstrate the surprising abundance of nice, comfy, cozy available wins vs. the spread by the margin of at least two touchdowns plus one extra point and one two-point conversion. This type of result is destined to happen an average of about once every 3.6 to 3.9 games.

Naturally, somebody's comfy, cozy win is always someone else's hapless defeat, and you don't want to be that someone else. This chapter probably should come with a caveat of "Don't Try This at Home" until you have practiced it hundreds of times. But now that we know that lopsided margins vs. the spread are out there to be had, let's hold these 15-point games under a microscope to see if they share any common factors that might make it easier to identify the eventual windshields and bugs.

In the three-year span from 2005 to 2007, 210 NFL games were decided by 15 points or more vs. the spread. Of those, 120 of them (57.1 percent) involved at least one of the head coaches being in his first or second season. Since in any given season, the number of Year One and Year Two head coaches will represent only about 40 percent of the existing tenures, the presence of at least one of them in 57 percent of the blowouts of this size is noteworthy.

Because new head coaches are usually replacing ones who were fired or retired, they are frequently left with one of two extremes: an empty cupboard, or a team whose management believed that the talent potential was not being maximized by the prior regime. Some new tasks appear hopeless in the short-term, as did Bobby Petrino's in 2007. In Petrino's case, a first-season head coach who was hired to jump-start the offense with more passing had hired inexperienced coordinators, and lost both quarterbacks from the prior season before their first season in Atlanta would begin. Five times in 2007, including Opening Day, the Falcons were blown out by 15 points or more vs. the spread. During a short Monday-to-Sunday week leading up to the fifth blowout defeat of drastic proportions at Tampa Bay, Petrino quit and was introduced as the new head coach at the University of Arkansas. On the same day, offensive coordinator Hue Jackson was spotted in Durham, North Carolina interviewing to be the head coach of Duke University. (Jackson didn't get the job but later became an assistant with the Ravens.) That rare situation in Atlanta—change of command on a downtrodden team with a temporary leader elsewhere—was a terrific indication of another "no-show" effort to come from a team that had already put forth four of them. I know someone—the guy who shaves in my mirror every other morning—who capitalized on that opportunity.

But when there is talent on hand and the players are willing to change, a new head coach, with the help of his new assistants and few personnel tweaks, can totally change a system and get drastic improvement that keeps opposing coaches one step behind in their preparation. The 2006 New Orleans Saints, on the way to 10 wins, recorded six 15 Pointers vs. the spread for Year One head coach Sean Payton. However, in Year Two in 2007, the exposure from 2006 cost the Saints and anyone who went chasing their successes from the prior season. The 2007 New Orleans Saints recorded five –15 Pointers vs. the spread in losses! This Year Two team was the poster boy for blowout-potential volatility, with nine of their sixteen games as 15-Pointers vs. the spread either way.

Year One Positive to Year Two Negative has an alter-ego: Year One Negative to Year Two Positive. Sometimes the drastic positive change doesn't happen until

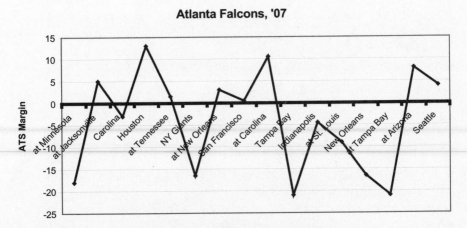

FIGURE 11-2 Atlanta Falcons, '07

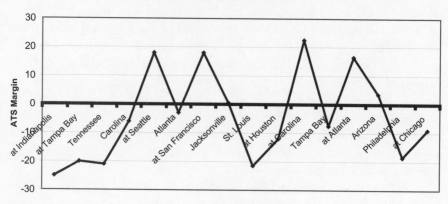

FIGURE 11-3 New Orleans Saints, '07

the new coach's second season, after he, his staff, and the team have had time to experience changes and learn to function better as they go along. The 2007 Green Bay Packers were an excellent example of that particular phenomenon in the second-season regime of head coach Mike McCarthy. Year One wasn't a disaster at 8-8 ATS, but Year Two results were as if the Packers were riding rockets on the way to covering the spread thirteen times.

Because of the related instabilities—which include inaccurate or incorrect general perceptions by the outside world—Year One and Year Two always carry the potential to be the most volatile for such teams on a game-by-game basis, creating fertile ground for blowouts either way. When the 2007 New England Patriots began their 16-0 SU season, they pulled off three straight 15-Pointers to start the season, all against teams with Year One or Year Two coaching regimes attempting to combat New England's relative stability within. Eventually, five of the Patriots' six winning 15-Pointers came against Year One or Year Two opponents. When those kinds of worlds collide, the potential exists for the more stable organization to be doing the blowing while the immature side, for lack of a more descriptive term, does the sucking.

Sometimes, a game with a final score of 34-14 is confused with being a blowout, on the basis of the final score margin of 20 points. But that mistake—a common error made by Straight-Up Man—forgets about the point-spread. If a −10 favorite won the game, they covered by 10 points. No blowout. If the +10 underdog won that game, they covered by +30 points. Blowout! The frequency of victorious 15 Pointers is much less among NFL double-digit favorites. Only 13.9 percent of all favorites −10 or higher have registered winning 15-Pointers in the 15 years spanning 1993 to 2007. Compare that to

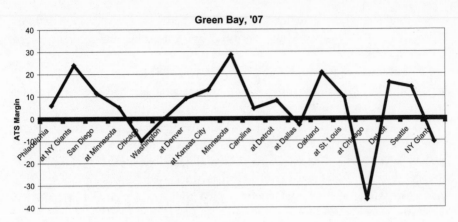

FIGURE 11-4 Green Bay Packers, '07

the 23.2 percent of all favorites of exactly −3 that have engineered favorable 15-Pointers. The disparity on display in this fact helps illustrate several points repeated in other chapters:

- The size of the spread does not determine how close the result will be vs. the spread.
- Oddsmakers and bookmakers are overrated and there are inversely proportional relationships between the size of the lines they make, and the margins of the results that take place against those lines.

If being a highly functioning member of ATS World wasn't all about attempting to predict unpredictability, one might say that blowouts are unpredictable. They do just sort of happen, but in a manner that severe weather just sort of happens in an unstable atmosphere. The average person doesn't see it, but a meteorologist makes his living tracking it, doesn't he? That is why we know that unstable air masses have the potential to create spontaneous convection currents which lead to cloud formation and storms. Same concept in football blowouts. The unstable conditions lead to tricky forecasting, which is why weatherman always says something like, "60 percent chance of rain." But the storms are not impossible to predict, and if you predict 60 percent successfully in football, you'll be making money.

Of course, meteorology requires a college degree. For successful NFL forecasting, you need to create your own courses and study like crazy just to be in position to make substance-laden forecasts that aren't merely opinions. Another common mistake made by Straight-Up Man is assuming blowout wins by a big favorite with apparent motivation to really "stick it" to the other team. But any coach of a large underdog who fears being blown out badly can plan to make it close, avoid losing, and actually put his team in better position to win by adopting what Smokin' Willy, a Midwestern football forecasting maven, likes to call "mouse" tactics.

"Not all cats are fat and happy," says Smokin'. "There are plenty of fat and happy mice living in the shadows eating nice, tasty cheese because they learned how to avoid being caught and dismembered by the cat."

In December of '07, you couldn't swing a dead cat in a New York sports bar without hitting someone who would say "75-0" in response to the question: "What do you think the final score of New England vs. the Jets will be?" Even poor Jets fans were convinced that the Patriots, who were ratted on by Jets' head coach Eric Mangini for illegal sideline videotaping after their first meeting of the season, were going to rub it in, retaliating in high-profile splendor for the NFL's subsequent $500,000 fine levied against head coach Bill Belichick, and loss of a future number one draft pick.

The 75-0 knee-jerkers were not aware that blowouts really cannot be planned for in the NFL, given the parity of talent between teams. If an NFL offense attempts to throw a touchdown pass on every play, it has a better chance of getting the quarterback sacked and injured, losing a fumble, being intercepted, and setting up the underdog for momentum-turning action that can snowball against the favorite.

Also, in games with a big line, you need to make sure whether or not the game is actually a high-priority for the favorite before making a selection that banks on the favorite bringing its "A" game to the table. On that day, the Patriots' eventual post-season destinations—home as long as they would last, then Phoenix for the Super Bowl—were all but inked. Still, the local New York media was adding fuel to the already hot rivalry:

> *There is nothing, absolutely nothing, the Jets can tape, scheme for, or say that will save them from being on the losing end of one of the most lopsided games in recent NFL history.*

Those were the words of a female sportswriter in *Newsday*. She never played the game, apparently never studied the game, yet felt qualified to explain with "absolute" certainty about how something that probably could not happen was nevertheless about to take place.

Even if the need to "play hard all the way" is there for the huge, supposedly mean and nasty favorite, you still have to realize that any opposing underdog coach at this level who fears being blown out can plan against it a lot better than the favored coach can plan for it. That is how Bill Belichick himself, as defensive coordinator of the New York Giants, helped beat Joe Montana and Jim Kelly on successive Sundays in 1990 to win the NFC Championship Game and Super

Bowl. When an underdog takes the always available option of committing to keep the play in front of them and funnel the action to the middle of the field on defense, and on offense waits until the last two seconds of the play-clock to snap the ball, and call plays that tend to stay in bounds to shorten the game, it makes a lopsided, embarrassing result less likely to occur. It also frustrates the huge favorite by forcing its offense to be patient to score, and forcing its defense to play more plays than they want to play against either high-percentage short passes, or energy-sapping straight-ahead runs.

The huge favorite will need to recover fumbles, make interceptions, and get defensive and special teams scores to run up the score. But when the big underdog is running "safe" plays, the likelihood of acquiring turnovers decreases. In the NFL, a 42-3 final score is not planned. A 42-3 final score usually happens when well-intentioned, aggressive plans are executed poorly and situations spiral out of control—like what was happening to the Detroit Lions (with a Year Two head coach Rod Marinelli) almost every other Sunday in 2007. The Lions lost four road games by –27 or –28 points vs. the spread, and another by –16 points vs. the number. Why? Throwing too often on offense. On defense, going for the big hit to try to force a fumble, or going for the big interception. Because they usually failed on both counts, it resulted in a parade of big plays against them made by the other team.

As it turned out in New York Jets at Foxborough, it was the huge –24 favorite New England that allowed a punt to be blocked and returned for a Jets' touchdown in soggy conditions. Anytime a huge favorite "stubs its toe," so to speak, and suffers an in-game implosion that gives the other side points, that huge favorite has little to no chance of covering the spread. The final score of 20-10 for New England was almost a blowout 15-pointer . . . for the supposedly hapless underdog Jets!

In his *Sports Illustrated* recap of the 1993 Super Bowl in which Buffalo turned it over nine times to Dallas in a 52-17 defeat, the incredible Dr. Z made this after-the-fact statement: "Turnovers are the heart of most NFL blowouts." Over the course of the next 15 years, few people have taken up the challenge of attempting to forecast this most influential factor on final margins and results vs. the spread.

12

Predicting Turnovers

I **N AUGUST OF** 2004, after a revealing discussion with someone who called himself a "professional handicapper," I realized a few things. One was that anyone could call himself a professional handicapper because with no credible criteria existing to judge it against, nobody will bother to challenge the assertion. The business of "professional handicappers," is loaded with Ed Wood types. Ed Wood was the low-budget movie director who hired Bela Lugosi's dentist to finish playing the vampire's role in *Plan 9 From Outer Space*, after Lugosi died during filming. Wood draped a cape around the guy, and shot him from "angles" that concealed his true identity as he lurked around the set.

Which I liken to someone anonymously scouring result logs for angles like: "Bears, 5-1 ATS last six! Go to the sports book and play it, where I will come to suck your blood!"

This particular "professional handicapper" was shrugging off a series of 48 percent winning seasons as simply a matter of bad luck. In making excuses, he sighed, "Well, you can't predict turnovers." To top it all off, he added that in his estimation, the NFL was "un-handicappable," and that if his dog could point to 60 percent winners, he'd resort to that method.

I was dumbstruck, and remember thinking, "Nice mindset, quitter. And you get paid for it?" I certainly wasn't ever going to pay him for it.

When interceptions and fumbles are as critical as they are to winning and losing—for the athletes as well as the wagerers—you had damn well better believe that turnovers can be predicted, then follow up on that belief with attempts to predict them. In a 2006 Monday Night game, all viewers with the sound on learned something very important about turnovers if they didn't know it already: In defensive huddles, the players stress the in-game turnover count! John Lynch, defensive captain of Denver, was commanding his teammates to get *two* turnovers to offset the one that the Broncos offense had already lost! Well, by game's end, the Broncos got *three*! That, in a nutshell, sums up why you had damn well better be prepared to predict a team's likelihood of making and committing turnovers. As surely as the offense is plotting for short gains and longer gains, the defense is plotting to get the ball back ASAP, if not by stopping the offense on downs and forcing a punt, then by taking the ball away whenever and wherever an opportunity exists. They're doing it, so you'd better be doing it, too.

I tell my NFL forecasting staff at *Sports Reporter* that their goals should be to write the Associated Press recap in their forecast. At first, they laugh. But eventually, the ones that remain on board with us "get it," shoot for it, and gain confidence when their insights make them stronger forecasters. The year after my discussion with the fake professional handicapper who couldn't or wouldn't predict turnovers, one of our newest staffers, Mike from San Francisco, penned this gem which, as usual, was published six days in advance:

Sports Reporter

NFL Week 13, 2005

CHICAGO(–7) over GREEN BAY by 10

A combination of stingy defensive play, an offense that focuses on field position, and their fair share of lucky bounces has helped the rejuvenated Bears compile an 8-3 record and an uncontested grasp on first place in the NFC North. Brett Favre's Packers . . . have suffered several devastating injuries-the latest to TE Bubba Franks—Green Bay's season-long woes can be tied into the ineffectiveness of an offensive line that lost two Pro Bowl-caliber stalwarts at guard to free agency. The fearsome front four of the Bears defensive line will give the Packers more than they can handle, and should effectively pressure Favre into increasing his league-leading total of interceptions, courtesy of Tillman, Vasher, and company. CHICAGO, 20-10.

The Associated Press recap writer had the easy job, explaining what happened with the advantage of having watched the action playing out before his eyes:

CHICAGO (AP)—The Bears roughed up Brett Favre with their defense. They knocked him down, intercepted two of his passes and beat the Green Bay Packers at Soldier Field for the first time since 1993 . . . Charles Tillman and Nathan Vasher had game-changing interceptions against Favre, who completed 31 of 58 passes for 277 yards against a team he had dominated over the years. Tillman returned the first interception just before halftime 95 yards to set up one of Robbie Gould's four field goals, and Vasher took a late interception 45 yards to seal the 19-7 victory . . .

So, what was that nonsense about turnovers being unpredictable?

Year	Team	TO Mar	W	L	T	ATS%	Avg Line
2007	San Diego	+24	11	5	0	68.8%	-5.2
2005	Cincinnati	+24	8	7	1	53.3%	-3.8
2005	Denver	+20	11	4	1	73.3%	-3.8
2004	Indianapolis	+19	9	6	1	60.0%	-5.3
2003	Kansas City	+19	10	6	0	62.5%	-5.9
2007	Indianapolis	+18	9	6	1	60.0%	-6.5
2004	NY Jets	+17	8	7	1	53.3%	-2.7
2003	New England	+17	13	2	1	86.7%	-1.3
2006	Baltimore	+17	10	6	0	62.5%	-2.5
2007	New England	+16	9	6	1	60.0%	-14.1
2005	Carolina	+16	10	6	0	62.5%	-3.9
2007	Tampa Bay	+15	9	7	0	56.3%	-0.8
2004	San Diego	+15	13	1	2	92.9%	0.6
2006	St. Louis	+14	8	7	1	53.3%	0.6
2003	Tennessee	+13	8	8	0	50.0%	-4.1
2006	San Diego	+13	9	7	0	56.3%	-6.8
2004	Carolina	+12	10	6	0	62.5%	0.5
2005	Indianapolis	+12	9	6	1	60.0%	-8.6
2004	St. Louis	-24	5	10	1	33.3%	-1.6
2005	New Orleans	-24	5	10	1	33.3%	4.4
2005	Green Bay	-24	6	9	1	40.0%	2.0
2006	Oakland	-23	6	9	1	40.0%	7.0
2004	San Francisco	-19	6	10	0	37.5%	5.8
2007	Baltimore	-17	3	13	0	18.8%	1.2
2004	Oakland	-17	6	10	0	37.5%	2.8
2004	Miami	-17	7	9	0	43.8%	5.0
2003	NY Giants	-16	3	11	2	21.4%	0.6
2003	Buffalo	-16	6	8	2	42.9%	0.0
2006	Cleveland	-15	6	8	2	42.9%	4.5
2004	Dallas	-15	7	9	0	43.8%	1.3
2004	Green Bay	-14	7	9	0	43.8%	-1.7
2003	Arizona	-13	6	10	0	37.5%	7.1
2007	Houston	-13	7	8	1	46.7%	2.2
2007	San Francisco	-12	5	10	1	33.3%	5.6
2006	Tampa Bay	-12	6	9	1	40.0%	4.6
2004	Cleveland	-12	6	10	0	37.5%	5.5

(Continued)

Figure 12-1 (*Continued*)

Year	Team	TO Mar	W	L	T	ATS%	Avg Line		Year	Team	TO Mar	W	L	T	ATS%	Avg Line
2005	NY Giants	+11	10	5	1	66.7%	-2.5		2007	Kansas City	-11	6	9	1	40.0%	3.8
2005	Jacksonville	+11	9	5	2	64.3%	-2.8		2005	Arizona	-11	6	10	0	37.5%	2.2
2004	Baltimore	+11	9	7	0	56.3%	-2.2		2007	Oakland	-11	6	10	0	37.5%	5.2
2003	San Francisco	+11	7	7	2	50.0%	-0.6		2003	San Diego	-11	6	10	0	37.5%	3.8
2004	Pittsburgh	+11	11	5	0	68.8%	-1.7		2003	Cleveland	-11	6	10	0	37.5%	2.5
2003	Minnesota	+11	8	7	1	53.3%	-2.2		2007	St. Louis	-10	5	11	0	31.3%	5.1
2007	Seattle	+10	9	7	0	56.3%	-4.1		2005	St. Louis	-10	6	10	0	37.5%	0.4
2003	Indianapolis	+10	9	6	1	60.0%	-3.7		2005	Baltimore	-10	7	9	0	43.8%	1.2
2004	Buffalo	+10	11	5	0	68.8%	-0.7		2005	San Francisco	-9	8	8	0	50.0%	9.7
2005	Seattle	+10	8	8	0	50.0%	-4.4		2007	NY Giants	-9	10	6	0	62.5%	-1.3
2004	New England	+9	11	3	2	78.6%	-6.8		2004	Tampa Bay	-9	5	9	2	35.7%	0.6
2007	Buffalo	+9	9	6	1	60.0%	5.4		2004	Denver	-9	6	7	3	46.2%	-4.5
2003	Jacksonville	+9	11	5	0	68.8%	-1.7		2003	Chicago	-9	8	7	1	53.3%	4.1
									2006	Detroit	-9	5	11	0	31.3%	3.9

* *NFL, 2003-2007*

FIGURE 12-1

Turnovers—losing the ball to your opponent via the gross errors known as interceptions and fumbles—are thought to be more costly to a team when committed near the team's own goal line. But in reality, no matter where they are committed, a turnover on average is worth about –4 points to the team making one, and +4 points to the team acquiring one. How much are turnovers worth vs. the point-spread? Check out the Top 30 and Bottom 30 Turnover Margin teams from the NFL over the course of a four-year period for an overview:

Yow! Among teams with the 31 best positive Turnover Ratios, only two lost money vs. the spread. At 50 percent ATS, those two teams were not disastrous investments. Among teams with the 32 worst Turnover Ratios, only two were profitable vs. the spread. The 2007 New York Giants, 10-6 ATS, NFC champions, and Super Bowl XLII winners despite a –9 Turnover Ratio, were pretty much the exception that proves the rule! Teams that turn it over the most and don't get it back enough are prime candidates to lose money vs. the spread. Teams that hang onto the ball the best and take it away the most are prime candidates to be profitable vs. the spread. Rely on a team with a very bad Turnover Ratio, and you delve into very risky territory. Keep your rosary beads and prayer book handy. Rely on a team with a very good Turnover Ratio, and be better positioned to win.

An exceptional defense creates turnovers. A sloppy offense commits turnovers. When Team A has the exceptional defense and is playing against Team B's sloppy offense, and Team A gets a lead, Team B is in trouble the larger the deficit becomes. Their plays become more predictable as the game-clock ticks away, increasing the chances for a turnover to be made because the defense can afford to gamble when it knows what's coming. An exceptional, takeaway oriented defense with a lead is like an expert card-counter in Las Vegas. When they have a good idea of what is about to come up, they can afford to gamble strongly. Also, by making second efforts to gain desperate yards, Team B's offensive players have a greater chance to put themselves in position to lose a fumble while trying too hard to make that comeback.

Exceptional defenses, it should be noted, can also acquire turnovers against good offenses. The 2007 San Diego Chargers led the NFL with 30 interceptions during the regular season. The next-highest interception count was 22. In *Sports Reporter* that season, we published three Best Bets on the Chargers when they faced the two best quarterbacks in the NFL, the superstar quarterbacks who had been compiling the best Touchdown to Interception Ratios: Peyton Manning and Tom Brady. The Chargers won two of the three games outright, covering the spread in all three. They intercepted Manning six times in one of the games, got three interceptions from him in the re-match, then picked Brady three times in the very next game.

Inexperienced quarterbacks, quarterbacks with a history of throwing interceptions, and quarterbacks playing for stubborn, pass-happy offensive coordinators, are more prone to throwing interceptions. Before the 2007

NFL regular season, Detroit Lions quarterback Jon Kitna publicly predicted that the Lions would win 10 games. This was a great example of why players should just play, coaches should just coach, and predictors should predict. Kitna, with ten NFL seasons under his belt including six as a starter, had career numbers of 147 TD passes and 146 interceptions. That was a horrible split, compared to Brady's 197-86, Manning's 306-153, and even Carson Palmer's 104-63, Palmer being the younger guy who had replaced Kitna as the starter in Cincinnati. To compound his problem, Kitna was playing for offensive coordinator Mike Martz, whose offenses traditionally passed more frequently and threw more interceptions. In 2001, Martz was the head coach and offensive brainpower of the Rams, who made it to the Super Bowl despite committing an NFL-high 44 turnovers. If the St. Louis defense hadn't pitched in with an NFL-high 34 turnovers acquired, the team never would have made it that far. The 2002 Rams turned it over 45 times, once again the most in the NFL. When the defense couldn't keep pace and acquired "only" 26 turnovers, the resulting −19 TO Ratio plunged the Rams to 4-12 ATS and out of the post-season.

When we heard Kitna's prediction, which he actually upgraded after the Lions drafted a wide receiver named Calvin Johnson with their first pick, then analyzed his history and Martz's tendencies, we had a bust in the making and projected it in our *Zone Blitz*:

> *Kitna thinks that a wide receiver—who needs to get the ball from a goof like himself and who will only touch it about 6 times per game—will make a huge difference in Detroit's play when the team first needs performance on the offensive and defensive lines to improve drastically. Recent wide receivers as first-round draft picks have included: Mark Clayton (Baltimore), Braylon Edwards (Cleveland), Lee Evans (Buffalo), Larry Fitzgerald (Arizona), Santonio Holmes (Pittsburgh), Matt Jones (Jacksonville), Roddy White (Atlanta), and Reggie Williams (Jacksonville). Four of those teams lost money vs. the spread in their rookie seasons, the other four made money vs. the spread, and none of them won a post-season game. Obviously, the rest of the team needs to be able to do more than the average share around a potentially-great wide receiver . . . When Kitna coughs it up, opponents can smash-mouth the Detroit defense to the goal line and beyond.*

The Lions passed on 64.6 percent of offensive downs, the NFL's strongest pass frequency of the season. Kitna's 2007 TD-to-INT ratio in 2007 was 17-22. Lions quarterbacks were sacked 54 times (league-worst was 55, best was 16) for −20 yards per game (league-worst was −23, best was −6), fumbled 16 times and lost 6. The Lions' defense acquired fewer turnovers (17) than Kitna's personal interception count. Detroit won only seven games—one in the last eight—and finished 7-8-1 ATS.

•   •   •

FUMBLES TEND TO be more costly than interceptions. On average, a fumble results in more than twice as many lost yards of field position as an interception. That is because interceptions usually involve the offense throwing the ball down-field for a "gain" before possession is lost, whereas fumbles tend to take place near the line of scrimmage. Naturally, an interception returned for a touchdown can have a drastic effect on momentum. But in general and on average, fumbles are worse.

"The other team's quarterback must go down, and he must go down hard." Those words of wisdom from Oakland Raiders' owner Al Davis—the last intelligible thing the man might have ever said—have always helped to emphasize what is potentially the strongest game- and season-changing dynamic in football.

Battered quarterbacks create a domino effect against a team and its bettors:

- Nobody at any of the skill positions is getting his yards or moving the chains when the quarterback is being buried. Punts must be resorted to more frequently.
- At the very least, a sack is a negative yardage play creating a more difficult down-and-distance situation for the very next play. An increase in down-and-distance difficulty makes the next play easier for the defense to figure out, which increases the chances for an interception: a turnover.
- At its near-worst, a quarterback going down hard results in a fumble: a turnover.

Absolute worst-case scenario is when the quarterback happens to be injured when sacked. The reserve QB is nearly always a drop-off in talent that requires an in-game adjustment—not easily accomplished—by everyone involved in the offense. And, the backup quarterback is more likely to fumble the snap or throw an interception.

When a mediocre team goes through a season with a drastically lower number of fumbles and lost fumbles by its quarterbacks, you can consider it a bad omen for the next season. In 2006, Daunte Culpepper, Joey Harrington, and Cleo Lemon combined to fumble only 7 times, losing only 1 in 16 games. Their quarterback fumble frequency was drastically lower than Oakland's 19-9, or Buffalo's 19-8 from the prior season. The median numbers were 10-6. But Miami was just a 6-win team that season, 6-10 ATS. Other negative issues offset clean play at the quarterback position. The following season, with a new, offensive-minded head coach Cam Cameron, Miami quarterbacks combined for 15-8 in fumbles. They fumbled more than twice as often, and lost eight times as many as the year before! The numbers themselves may not have appeared poor on the surface. But in a short season, there is no time to recover from such trauma, especially when the frequencies are so much higher than the prior year, the team's starting power rating is partly a function of the good ball safety from the prior year, and they stink in general. The 2007 Dolphins suffered a 1-win season and covered only 5 times vs. the spread.

Part of the skill of forecasting turnovers is also assessing when they will *not* happen. In other words, recognizing bad luck from the past, and the strong possibility for pending improvement in overall offensive cohesion. In other chapters, it has been noted how the 2006 New Orleans Saints cleaned up their act after a new head coach booted the old quarterback following a season of 83 percent fumble losses. Removing the fumble- and turnover-prone quarterback Aaron Brooks from their equation was a big factor in erasing the mess. The same scenario took place in favor of the Cleveland Browns in 2007, as mentioned in another chapter. After the old, turnover-prone quarterback Charlie Frye was removed, his replacement put fewer stains on the carpet. When your host keeps a clean house, it's always a pleasure to be there. From the moment Frye was removed, Cleveland went 12-2-1 ATS. But the fact of the matter was that by virtue of having been on the extreme unlucky side of the fumbles-lost scale the year before, they had very real potential to post an over-the-top point-spread record by virtue of having been de-valued to an unrealistic point. There isn't a dog in the world that can grasp that fact and point to it.

13
Positioning for Upsets

AS FIGURE 13-1 (from 1993–2007) clearly illustrates, there is a relatively steady and proportional relationship between underdog size, and frequency of straight-up victories by underdogs. The fewer points taken by the underdog, the greater the straight-up win frequency. Underdogs of about a field goal have won about 40 percent of their games, underdogs of about a touchdown show a 25 percent win frequency. The declining win-frequency pattern actually flattens out as the point-spread increases to the +8 to +10 range, where the historical frequency of outright wins has been between 22 percent and 24 percent.

As the size of the NFL underdog increases beyond a field goal, an outright win by that team is generally considered to be an "upset."

But it's only an upset if you buy the hype. Think about it. If, after doing your homework, you believe that an underdog can or will win the game, then a win by that team is not a surprise to you. It's only a surprise to people who didn't see it coming, and it upsets their own personal applecart more than it upsets anything else. An underdog is an underdog only by virtue of the betting line's existence, and the betting line is comprised of data from the past that is not guaranteed to be indicative of future results.

The terms "underdog" and "favorite" do not appear in NFL team playbooks. Those terms are part of a language spoken only by oddsmakers, bookmakers and bettors, where the need to communicate balanced action drives and sustains the market. Broadcast producers and commentators, who carry a mandate to sell the sizzle, not the steak, also speak this language. "Year after year, some headline writers need to be taken to the woodshed," said Joe Hofmann, a sportswriter for the *Daily Record* of Hackensack, New Jersey who "gets it" and has seen more than his share of over-hyping and overreaction. Dan LeBatard of the *Miami Herald* also has his perspective straight. "There is really no such thing as an upset any more in the NFL given that the financial system is structured to legislate balance and parity."

Line	W	L	Pct.
0	52	52	50.0%
+1, 1.5	86	82	51.2%
+2, 2.5	236	266	47.0%
+3, 3.5	284	429	39.8%
+4, 4.5	206	340	37.7%
+5, 5.5	47	107	30.5%
+6, 6.5	157	339	31.7%
+7, 7.5	74	204	26.6%
+8, 8.5	62	217	22.2%
+9, 9.5	27	92	22.7%
+10, 10.5	56	178	23.9%
+11, 11.5	8	46	14.8%
+12, 12.5	13	67	16.3%
+13, 13.5	5	33	13.2%
+14, 14.5	18	59	23.4%
+15, 15.5	0	14	0.0%
+16, 16.5	0	23	0.0%
+17, 17.5	0	7	0.0%
+18, 18.5	1	8	11.1%
+19, 19.5	0	1	0.0%
+20, 20.5	0	2	0.0%
+21, 21.5	0	1	0.0%
+22, 22.5	0	1	0.0%
+23, 23.5	0	1	0.0%
+24, 24.5	0	2	0.0%

FIGURE 13-1 SU Wins by NFL underdogs

Very few NFL underdogs enter a game envisioning defeat. If the players don't already know what the line is, the coaches will use the point-spread as a motivational tool to help rally the troops in an attempt to make the goal of winning seem like a greater achievement. "Nobody believes we can do it!"

In ATS World, there really is no difference between a +7 underdog that wins by 3 points, and a −10 favorite that wins by 20. Yet Joe Public doesn't run around screaming about a remarkable upset when a −10 favorite wins 34-14, even though the net result is the same.

In both instances, however, each winning side—the +3 underdog and the −10 favorite—are accomplishing the exact same thing by bettering the spread by 10 points. The spread, and the performance against it, is the only thing that should interest an ATS Man. Therefore, the best way to position for upsets is to stay on track with themes being hammered home throughout this book. Don't go out looking for upsets. Let them come to you. Talent, preparation, matchup exploitation, performance, and execution on the field determine winning and losing. When you think one team owns edges in enough areas against the rest, or owns a single, solitary edge that it can ride throughout the game, you'll be selecting that team because you think it can outperform the line—the line which is always right—by a couple of scores. The line is really irrelevant. Therefore, there is no such thing as an upset. You could pick any season, sort out the straight-up wins by +7 or greater underdogs, and give very sound reasons why that side could have won the game. Let's look back at a few 2007 match-ups.

Week 1

Tennessee Titans +7.5 at Jacksonville (13-10)

The game took place right after the Jaguars had cut loose starting quarterback Byron Leftwich and promoted David Jaguars Garrard. Besides the sudden quarterback change, the favored Jaguars also had a few *offensive linemen* injured and out, as well as a *new offensive coordinator calling plays for the first time in an NFL game* after coming from the college ranks. There was a *learning curve* to hurdle in key spots. Tennessee was not as talented, but the Titans were actually the more stable team on that day.

Week 2

Cleveland +7 vs. Cincinnati (51-45)

First of all, the underdog was home, and one of the first things we established in this book is that *home teams win 60 percent of all NFL games*. Because Cleveland had lost 34-7 on Opening Day vs. Pittsburgh, there were immediate negative public perceptions about the Browns based on the prior week. But last week was last week. A *quarterback change* was also involved here, with the "underdog" Cleveland team making a publicized switch from Charlie Frye to Derek Anderson. Cincinnati didn't know much about Anderson and was coming off a nationally televised win on Monday Night—*traveling off a short week and a win*, always a red flag on a favorite. Cleveland's *offensive coordinator was new, too*. An underdog with a new offensive coordinator represents more trouble to the favorite, whose systems are more familiar to the underdog.

Week 2

Houston +7 at Carolina, (34-21)

Would Carolina be slightly distracted by what was on the horizon for them? The next three weeks would be *a wave of games against NFC South Division rivals Atlanta, Tampa Bay, and New Orleans*. A bad start to division play can doom a team's season early (Carolina would go on to win two of the next three). Houston, with knowledge that they are the fourth-best team in a tough AFC South with Indianapolis, Jacksonville, and Tennessee all winning from 9 to 12 games the prior season, would need to place an emphasis on non-division and non-conference games because achieving merely 3-3 within their division would be next to impossible (they eventually went 1-5 SU against the division, 7-3 SU elsewhere.) Carolina was in *early transition to a new run-blocking scheme on the offensive line*, a system in place at only three other NFL teams. *Houston* was one of those teams, and the Texans had a full season head start on it against the Panthers, having started it in 2006 in head coach Gary Kubiak's first season. Carolina rushed for only 53 yards despite jumping out to a 14-7 lead. Matt Schaub, *the new Houston quarterback, had prepped in practice twice a year for three seasons against Carolina as a backup for the Atlanta Falcons.*

• • •

YOU COULD GO on and on and decipher factors that were at work enabling every so-called "upset." But they are essentially the same factors that eventually lead to scoreboard separation between two teams in any game at any pre-determined line. In Chapter 2, we already established that objectives of NFL teams and point-spread players are two different things. When a +13 underdog loses a game by 3 points, it's a loss for the team's purposes. If that +13 underdog loses by 21 points and does not cover the spread, to them it is the same as losing by 3 points and covering the spread. Close, but no cigar. It earns an "L," in the standings regardless of the supreme effort and the narrow losing margin. There is no such thing as a moral victory. They feel bad. It's a wasted week unless they learned something from the effort that can be put to use in later games. But anyone with a bet on them at +13 is a winner, because the teams and the bettors have two completely different agendas.

The largest outright underdog winner of the 2005 season was the Buffalo Bills, +14 at Cincinnati in Week 16. The Bengals were coming off a 41-17 win that clinched the AFC North division title and the team's first playoff berth in 15 years! "The Bengals put on a clinic yesterday," said one media source, placing them on the ol' precarious pedestal. Buffalo was 5-10 SU, long since eliminated from the playoffs. But with Cincinnati off the landmark achievement and feeling way too good about it, they were about to go from clinic-givers to woodshed-walloped in the span of one game. The "underdog" Bills pulled everything out of their bag of tricks—a flea-flicker, an onsides kick, a reverse on a kickoff return. "We just . . . threw it all at 'em. I felt like we had to put some points on the board any way we could," said Buffalo's head coach Mike Mularkey.

For a team's form to sustain itself, all eleven men on the field must be on point on nearly every play. If not, that team has a great chance to lose, by varying degrees of margins. A so-called underdog rarely wins because of bulletin-board material. But it can win because of the combined effects of its own intensified commitment and a situation-induced letdown by the favorite. It can win because they want it that much more, prepare accordingly, practice that much harder, and execute well against a favorite that doesn't account well enough for what the underdog might do.

The Bills bettered the spread by 24 points that day against the Bengals. But despite being the biggest so-called "underdog" upset of 2005, Buffalo's win was only the 19th largest spread-beater of the season. Eighteen other teams, 11 of them favorites, registered victories by more than 24 points vs. the spread. In a Week 5 home game, then 0-4 SU Green Bay (–3) beat New Orleans 52-3 to represent the season's largest margin vs. the spread (46 points). Ten weeks later in a road game, that same Green Bay (+3) team was on the losing side of the season's second-largest spread-beater in a 48-3 loss at Baltimore (42 points). In the lopsided win against New Orleans, Green Bay's Turnover Margin was 5-0. In the lopsided loss at Baltimore, the Packers' Turnover Margin was 0-5. It was a beautiful piece of leveling symmetry almost destined to happen to a Green Bay team that was just 3-10 SU at the time it faced Baltimore on the road late in the season on a Monday Night. Weren't the margins of these two games more remarkable than Buffalo's "upset" win at Cincinnati?

The largest outright underdog winner of the 2007 season was the St. Louis Rams, +13.5, at New Orleans in Week 10. At the time, early-season injuries and some blowout defeats had combined to seriously deflate St. Louis's power rating. On game-day, the Rams were 0-8 SU, 1-7 ATS. The Saints were on streak of 4-0 SU and ATS following a 0-4 SU and ATS start to the season. But the 0-4 ATS start to the season included three losses by more than 20 points vs. the spread, which proved that the Saints were perfectly capable of playing way below the expectations set by the point spread. As the NFL's only winless team, the Rams were the NFL's most desperate bunch leading into that game, and they had two weeks to prepare for it, with the assistance of their defensive coordinator Jim Haslett, the man who had been New Orleans's head coach from 2001 until he was fired after the 2005 season. After Sean Payton had further tarnished Haslett's reputation by leading the Saints to the NFC Championship Game as their first-season head coach in 2006, Haslett was the NFL's most desperate defensive coordinator on the

NFL's most desperate team, who owned an edge generally unseen by the public. Haslett was a coordinator who possessed intimate, locker room X and O knowledge of the opponent. As a man with pride who had been fired by the organization, he had an opportunity to get a measure of revenge with extra time to draw up and practice the plans for it. Do you think he'd make the most of it?

Haslett called blitzes on 16 of New Orleans's first 18 plays from scrimmage! "Defensively, I think they had a plan for us. They executed that plan very well," said losing New Orleans quarterback Drew Brees. "They did a great job of getting pressure and their offense really helped the defense out by staying on the field." And why wouldn't an opposing offense have done a great job of staying on the field against the New Orleans defense, which had been allowing, and would eventually allow, the most rushing plays per game in the NFL? A defense that cannot get off the field has no business being favored by −13.5 against anyone, not even a winless opponent.

St. Louis's 37-29 win as the NFL's largest outright-winning underdog ranked only 26th in margin vs. the spread in 2007. The largest spread-beater of 2007, by 39 points, was registered by the San Diego Chargers (+1) at Denver, 41-3. It came in Week 5 with San Diego off three consecutive defeats, and the know-it-alls calling for the head of new coach Norv Turner after the Chargers had been 14-2 SU in the prior regular season. The general public was surprised by the result, which was Denver's most lopsided home loss in 41 years. Yet the transparency of what was to come prompted this "Best Bet, San Diego" published in *Sports Reporter* six days before the game:

Best Bet

SAN DIEGO over DENVER

"When public outcry is at its peak, the point-spread, she is weak." Norv Landry, San Diego's living legend and master 1-3 SU string-puller, has a message for his ex-colleague from the Miami Dolphins, current Denver defensive coordinator Jim Bates: "Dude, I know you and what you're trying to do on defense, and your guys can't do it successfully against us!"

New Orleans was facing an opponent that hadn't won in eight games; Denver hadn't lost by that much at home since 1966. Both were in position to be blown away in an astounding manner. They called one result an "upset," the other a "surprisingly easy" victory by the winner. No! When you know enough about the NFL and are on top of your game, those types of situations and results represent business as usual. There are no upsets. There are no surprises. Those two words are not in the language spoken by a certain, select population living in ATS World.

14

The Great Value Debate

O NE OF THE reasons sports books never die is that some of the heaviest players are pseudo-sophisticates. They like to bet. They haven't necessarily developed the will to win. They wager large sums and throw around the fancy term, "value," often citing half-point line moves as the trigger to value. Some assign the value to the side whose "cover" gets a half-point easier to achieve via the line move. Others attach the value to the side drawing the action, calling it "smart money."

Do they really understand what constitutes value? Given that a value can be an ambiguous concept that governs human behavior, does anyone wagering on the NFL really understand what value might be within this particular arena? In psychological circles, there is an entire "value theory" branch that studies how humans develop, assert and believe in certain values, and how they act or fail to act on them. These values are considered to be very subjective.

Value has the potential to be a very over-played, misunderstood term. Lots of bettors believe value lies within the point-spread. But the point-spread isn't performing. The teams are performing against it, and the objective is to find teams or the totals that will out-perform the line by the greatest margin.

As cited in an earlier chapter, Coca-Cola—or any soda—is a great example of how value is misinterpreted. If a brand of soda is on sale for less money than other brands, someone will buy it via the judgment that the lowest price represents value against the other brands. Very often, that person will be required to buy a minimum number of units to qualify for the discounted price. This ensures that they and their loved ones are destined to consume mass quantities of a product that can lead to obesity and other sugar-related health disorders, and has no benefits other than satisfying the addiction to sugar that it originally created within its victim, er, consumer. There is nothing that a person needs in soda that wasn't already in their tap water. Does anyone need the sweet taste of soda to quench a thirst? No. Of course not. But they've been conned into thinking that they do. A regular consumer of soda who would pay only one cent per bottle wouldn't be getting any real value, because of the negative effects of the product over time. Diet soda? Come on, anyone who believes that con is also too far gone to be helped.

Point-spreads create the same sorry perception of value. A lot of people think that the greater the point-spread for an underdog, the greater the value. "Oh, they can lose by 13 points and still cover! That favorite doesn't have to win by 14 points to win the game. Atlanta is the value here!" Then, that bettor takes +14 with Atlanta because of the perceived generous price. Atlanta loses by 24. Was there ever really any value in Atlanta, +14? Hell, no. Warren Buffett, one of the most successful investors in America, said, "Price is what you pay, value is what you get."

Value is usually unseen, which is why it's hard to define. Maybe the best way to explain value in the NFL is to cite some examples of how the people at *Sports Reporter* have interpreted value and communicated it to readers before the games were played:

Super Best Bet

SAN DIEGO (–7) over CHICAGO
Week 1, 2007—After scoring nine defensive and special teams touchdowns last season, the Bears are probably the most overvalued team in football.—Result: San Diego covers spread.

As discussed in Chapter Eight, extreme highs in favorable turnover ratios or special-teams production create lopsided scores that inflate a team's rating for when seasons change, and their luck changes along with it. When you make this sort of judgment, apply it early and succeed, you can file it for use in the near future, like this:

Best Bet

MINNESOTA (+5) over CHICAGO
Week 6, 2007—Shortly after he made his first staff hire in January '06, Vikings head coach Brad Childress made it very clear that it was "all about beating the Bears." The Bears are overvalued. They represent a lot of defensive and special teams inflation from the past that places their backers in the rather odd position of waiting for lightning from yesterday's storm to strike.—Result: Minnesota covers spread.

When you investigate and isolate a specific factor in advance, then see it coming, apply it, and capitalize upon it a few times, you have successfully uncovered and tapped into value.

Lopsided defeats create fear in "scoreboard" watchers, who are wary that they will be repeated by a team. They forget that as soon as the last game is final, the new score is 0-0 and the opponent is different. We hadn't forgotten that fact, as evidenced by this call two weeks earlier:

Recommended

DETROIT (–3) over TAMPA BAY by 11

Week 7, 2007—The Lions' coaches have two weeks to get ready for a team they know inside and out. Head coach Rod Marinelli and his first-season defensive coordinator Joe Barry launched themselves from Jon Gruden's Bucs staff and into their current Detroit positions. When the Lions lose in blowout fashion as they have on the road (56-21 and 34-3), they really create excellent value on themselves for targeted home games.-Result: Detroit wins, 23-16.

Correct detection of the hidden value within a "lopsided loser" was a theme we had already developed as a routine, as this example from the prior season demonstrated. The 49ers had lost games by scores of 41-0, 48-19, and 41-10 already and were playing the first-place team in their division:

Best Bet

SAN FRANCISCO (+4.5) over SEATTLE

Week 11, 2006—The Seahawks are a turf team coming to play on a grass surface that most visitors detest. Some lopsided, turnover-influenced losses have helped to create some value on the 49ers. Go for it while the taking is good.-Result: San Francisco wins outright, 20-14.

Locating and sitting on value requires a little contrarian analysis—a stock market approach that owes its name to the observation that investors, as a group, are usually wrong about the direction of the stock market. At the peaks of bull markets, for example, when people ought to be getting out of stocks, optimism tends to be widespread—and the prevailing belief is that happy days are here to stay. This is like an NFL team on a winning streak. "4-0 ATS!" Abrupt endings are always around the corner. At bear-market bottoms, by contrast, the mood is often gloom and doom, even though investors' best course would be to jump back into the stock market with both feet. Increasing pessimism—the kind that multiple, blowout losses creates—defines the so-called "wall of worry" that bull markets like to climb, in what a financial analyst for MarketWatch calls "the classic contrarian view."

When you scale that wall of worry successfully a few times, you gain the confidence that turns value-detecting into one of the easiest parts of this obstacle course called NFL wagering and forecasting. Alan Greenspan, Chairman of the U.S. Federal Reserve Board, the most advanced economic wizard of this era, once asked the question regarding the stock market: "How do we know when irrational exuberance has unduly escalated asset values?" He didn't have an answer. But by getting underneath the NFL and performing valid research to help develop a better understanding of why things tend to happen the way they do, you can uncover some secrets and improve your chances of correctly forecasting future results.

Part Three
The Tactical

15
Let the Games Come to You

O **NE OF THE** most important axioms in the ol' game of life is that failing to plan is planning to fail. Therefore, anyone who enters an NFL season without at least having a general game plan is being an impudent fool who thinks they are bigger than the game, and bigger than basic, proven principles to help achieve success regardless of the endeavor. Anyone who wants to wager and win on the NFL needs to first go through the workout. No walk-ons. Sure, you can play as a walk-on. But have you ever watched a college basketball game in the last 1:30 of the second half when the coach of the home team with a 24-point lead removes his starters and inserts the walk-ons? If you have, you know that they get outplayed, badly, often by the losing team's second-stringers, because they lack game experience.

You are your own coach in this thing, and if you don't establish your own spring mini-camps and summer training camp, the odds will always be against you being sharp enough to pick enough winners to make a positive difference. Most of the previous chapters shed light on what kind of workout research can be performed between seasons. The more you know beforehand, the less you need to know when the season begins, which facilitates the task of absorbing, filtering and prioritizing new information as it occurs. Lists of potential "On" and "Against" teams should be made way in advance—subject to revision as necessary. Individually-targeted games should also be circled way in advance—weeks, even months ahead of time. Targets can always be deleted if deemed necessary, and others will materialize down the road as games come and go and yield new criteria that demands your "due diligence," as Smokin' Willy likes to say.

The biggest irony about picking winners vs. the spread in the NFL is that anybody is eligible to try. A 10-year-old kid playing an entry in his dad's office pool can do it and win. A brain surgeon vacationing at a Laughlin, Nevada hotel can do it and lose. This is quite a contrast from the qualifications necessary to own or manage an NFL franchise, and the prerequisites of actually being a professional football player on an NFL team.

NFL players do not get to that level until they first complete from one to four years of college. To be able to play college football at a school deemed worthy by NFL scouts, players need to have invested at least two years in high school football. Many NFL players enter the league after already having played the game of football for 12 years at ascending levels of competence and competitiveness, gaining physical strength and maturity as well as football experience along the way.

Detectives don't get to solve cases unless they've completed four years of college with a Criminal Justice degree, or at least graduated from 30 weeks of police academy and then served at least two years on the force.

But what are the qualifications for attempting to pick NFL winners vs. the spread, which requires sharp football knowledge, dedicated research skills and mathematical adeptness? There are none! How ironic. The system is set up so that any twit with a $20 bill and an opinion can put money down on a side in an NFL game. There is an epidemic lack of respect for the amount of study time and resources necessary to be properly prepared to win.

The NFL regular season runs from September through December. There isn't a player or a coach who thinks he can sit on his butt from February to September, then suddenly show up on opening day for the first time, and have a good season. Yet for some unknown reason, NFL point-spread players—as a group—fail to grasp the crucial need to apply the same year-round discipline demanded of the athletes. They don't understand that since coaches begin preparing for the next season in February, and players engage in mini-camps in May and June prior to July summer camp and August exhibition season, that they, the point-spread players, need to put themselves on a similar training schedule. Anyone who shows up in September and starts betting with no foundation is destined to lose, unless that person is blessed with a whole lotta luck. But luck only holds out for so long. You cannot show a long-term disrespect for the process of picking winners without being burned badly. A quarterback does not take the field unless the coach is confident that he has a grasp of his own playbook, and how he should operate against the other team's defensive scheme. If you ever want to see what would happen to a quarterback with no prior training and minimal reps in the system, rent the movie *Paper Lion*, the account of late sportswriter George Plimpton's experiences leading up to one series as Detroit Lions quarterback in an exhibition game. He lost 32 yards on 4 plays. "The story I got," Plimpton would later tell *Time* magazine, "was one I couldn't have, if I had not marched onto the field and tried my best. Very humiliating."

Muscle memory—reps in the system—plays a huge part in the enhancement of your decision-making skills. Gaining experience and knowledge, then implementing it successfully, builds confidence. Confidence is one of the biggest keys to winning, but confidence is often confused with having a strong opinion. You don't want to have an opinion. You want to form a confident expectation of what is about to happen. Anyone can watch an NFL team perform poorly in a game and come to the conclusion: "This team sucks, and will get destroyed in their next game, too!" Anyone can then be eligible to place a bet against that team, following that strong hunch. But knee-jerk reactions are not part of a winner's profile.

Smokin' Willy has learned to curb his enthusiasm. In December 2007, the Chicago Bears plucked a +3 TO Ratio in a Monday Night Football game at Minnesota, yet still lost. The majority of +3 TO Margin teams will win their games. That's how bad the Bears looked that night. Within a more complicated qualifying package that targets next games off prior game events, Chicago's failure to win despite a +3 TO Ratio was one key criteria for Smokin' to be ready to play against. On deck for the Bears was Green Bay, 12-2 SU, 12-2 ATS for the season to that point. The matchup would feature legendary, prolifically productive quarterback Brett Favre against the Bears' third-string quarterback, Kyle Orton, who, in his effort vs. Minnesota, looked more like a junior high baton-twirler than an NFL quarterback.

"My concern with being anti-Bears," he said the next morning, "is that it was advertised to millions and the huge consensus will be anti-Bears. 'Oh, Minnesota played like doggie-doo, Bears have no quarterback, Green Bay is good, Bears suck. Thus, we must bet Green Bay!'

"Maybe. But I want to soak it in and think like a Bear for a bit. I want to make sure I'm not getting fat eating the same dwindling supply of cheese, especially if there is a rat in the supply room. If I had pegged Green Bay in this game vs. the Bears prior to last night, then it would probably be all go. But since I had not, I would only be reacting to what I saw. Yes, the Bears' turnover situation is a qualifier, but that is just a starting point. Due diligence must prevail. When the Bears are greater than a touchdown underdog, especially at home, it is entering new ground. I'm very, very picky when it comes to NFL."

This was a terrific example of being prepared and confident. His homework had already been done to produce Green Bay as a qualifier. But he was smart enough to know that just because his own "system," as it were, had landed the Packers in his lap against the Bears, he wasn't forced to accept it without checking it out first. Buyer beware.

Against the Packers, Orton completed only 8-of-14 passes for 101 yards. Yet Chicago (+8.5), off the embarrassing defeat, embarrassed the Packers by the score of 35-7! Sometimes, the best wagers are the ones you do not make.

• • •

WHEN AN NFL halfback takes a toss from the quarterback, that one particular portion of that one single play out of 60 plays executed by an offense in any given game is practiced at least 100 times a year, even though the two players involved have performed the same play with different teammates at different levels 1,000 times in their lives. But if that part of the play was practiced with any less frequency, then the chances of the football being tossed inaccurately or fumbled increases. It's all part of being a professional and maintaining peak performance.

Lots of bettors think that the simple act of placing bets represents an effort at developing muscle memory and getting reps in the system. This is why casinos and sports books never go out of business. An NFL bettor who doesn't adopt a program parallel to the athlete's program—tailored, of course, for the forecasting of outcomes—is unfit for the task of investing vs. the point-spread. After all, if you were drafting for an NFL Point-Spread Investing Team, would you select somebody whose resume said they did no homework until the season started?

Muscle memory is when an active person repeatedly trains movement, often of the same activity, in an effort to stimulate the mind's adaptation process. The desired outcome is to induce physiological changes which attain increased levels of accuracy through repetition. Picking winners for profit vs. the spread requires repetition of thought process: brain training. Just as physical prowess can be maintained and improved with regular exercise and workouts, brain power can be maintained and improved with regular stimulation. Again, many bettors consider the simple act of betting as their regular stimulation. That is the difference between pathological and professional approaches to doing this. The pathological way is, "Game coming, bets being accepted, opinion forced for the sake of action." The professional way is, "Let's see if I have anything circled in advance for this week, or if any situations have developed that can usually be capitalized upon."

Smokin' Willy has trained himself to make NFL investment decisions just like a quarterback is trained in the simultaneous physical/mental functions of throwing mechanics, and choosing an intended receiver. Like the quarterback's training, he trains himself to fine-tune the selection process to maintain competence and confidence. That type of player wastes less time agonizing over which side to pick, rarely changes his mind, and creates more productive time for himself.

"I tend to lay off the game more than reverse an original direction," he says. But I consciously think about that very situation—'switching'—then slap myself. When I'm tracking well, I see targets in advance, or see a trigger that I have confidence in that doesn't require me seeing a lot of collaborative data in agreement. When I'm in tune like that, I don't overanalyze or let other influences impact my original target reasoning."

"When I'm short on time, don't put in the hard work, I scramble and catch myself drifting back and forth on a side based on the latest piece of information

I uncover. Very similar to "picking with the eyes." Bad for me. Very, very bad. Unfortunately, it happens. But at least I know I'm doing it. That's how Joe Public makes his picks. Ultimately, if your style isn't working or you don't have confidence, it's either time to find something that is, or resort to prayer and listening to *SportsCenter*."

Smokin' says that when he talks to fellow wagerers, mainly recreational types, he notices a lack of advance planning. Life's daily responsibilities are numerous, eating away at focus time and creating distractions. Still, they like to bet. "This often compels them to react to what they have seen with their eyes, or on ESPN, or live at a game, or gravitate to their favorite teams. They won't necessarily be wrong, but the true gems among opportunities cannot be uncovered like that."

Nothing, he says, is ever automatic. "My targeted situations/occurrences show me where to focus my limited time," Smokin' says. "This is the main downfall in my opinion of 'situation' players. They should not be auto plays. If a certain situation is a historical 70 percent producer, then I want to put my energy on the 30 percent non-producing results." In that particular pool, Smokin' believes he might find something that others have yet to learn, spawning his own growth and advancement to new horizons. "I can take off and jump right back in because I have a basis of where to begin. I won't get fat and lazy and resort to my eyes for success, because that will make me a loser among all other losers."

One of the biggest mistakes an NFL bettor can make is to read annual NFL Preview magazines like *The Sporting News, Street and Smith's*, and *Athlon* that are released in July, and attempt to pass it off as preparation for the upcoming season. You are projecting, not previewing. Previews are a bunch of Straight-Up sportswriters picking NFL teams to finish 1-2-3-4 in their division. Which is why I consider them to have all the impact of a girl in high heels throwing a football. Being correct about picking an NFL team second in its division isn't much of an effort or an accomplishment when there are only four teams per division. It's a soft toss!

"They made the playoffs last year and should do so again," is an example of the depth of analysis you generally get in a preview magazine. Picking a team to make the playoffs doesn't do the point-spread player any justice, either. One out of every 2.4 NFL teams gets to the playoffs! You want to know whether the team figures to overvalued or undervalued. You want to know what might happen along the way based on events and statistical occurrences from the prior year and personnel, coaching, and schedule differences upcoming, and how you might be able to benefit from all of it. You don't want a preview. You want projections! Targets! Nobody says you have to fire at every target. Life is all about building options. You want to learn as much as possible in order to create as many options as possible in front of you to pick and choose from. One of your objectives is that no action is forced. You want to be like an experienced quarterback seeing the field in front of you. The kind of quarterback who, after the game, tells the sportswriter, "The game has really slowed down for me." That quarterback is in a zone because he prepared and practiced well. When the game is moving too quickly for a quarterback, two things happen: he makes mistakes that lead to losses, then he doesn't play at all. That's exactly what will happen to an unprepared NFL wagerer, who cannot play after he runs out of money.

You are the coach and the quarterback of your NFL playing field. Remember, only a bad coach allows a bad quarterback to keep playing. The following quotes were from six different NFL quarterbacks, with six different levels of accomplishment, made separately over a span of twenty-five years:

> *"All I do is just look at my progressions and just go from there. Just play the game and let the game come to me. So that is pretty much what I have been doing each week."*

> *"I have to be patient and let the game come to me, and play the game that I've been playing all these years."*

> *"I have to be very patient and let the game come to me."*

> *"Just kind of let the game come to me and don't worry about other things."*

> *"The one thing I've learned over time is to let the game come to me and try to make the play when it's there, instead of gambling by leaving my responsibility . . . because that's when you hurt the team."*

> *"From my own personal standpoint, I tried too hard to make every play . . . I didn't let the game come to me. I tried to force things."*

In the NFL, a quarterback is considered to be a very good asset if he completes 60 percent of his passes. A head coach can keep his NFL job for a long time, and make lateral moves elsewhere within the league, if he averages 60 percent wins (9.5 per regular season) plus some post-season wins on top of it. A point-spread investor who wins with 60 percent frequency while wagering the same amount on every game, will net a 14.5 percent return on the investment. By comparison, what kind of interest is your bank paying on CDs and Money Market accounts these days?

To let the game come to you, you have to be on top of your game. Many of the previous chapters have discussed how to stay in shape during the off-season. The workouts begin in February, right after the Super Bowl, six months before the next action takes place. Like the Nike ads say, "Just do it."

16

The Coaching Network

N **FL OWNERS AND** general managers are starting to get smart by holding head coaches and coordinators contractually bound to non-compete clauses. A non-compete clause—a tactic popular with employers in the real world outside the NFL—usually tries to prevent former employees from working for competitors of the employer for a specified period of time.

A non-compete clause in the NFL reportedly prevented Rex Ryan, 2007 defensive coordinator of the Baltimore Ravens, from becoming the 2008 defensive coordinator for the Washington Redskins, even though Ryan was let go along with the rest of Brian Billick's Baltimore staff at the end of the 2007 season. (Ryan was later re-hired by Baltimore's incoming head coach as assistant head coach/defensive coordinator). A vertical or downward move by a coordinator—to become a head coach or a position coach elsewhere—would normally not be a restriction within a non-compete clause.

The use of non-compete clauses is premised on the possibility that upon being fired or resigning, the employee might be hired by a competitor or start a business, and gain competitive leverage by using—perhaps abusing—intimate knowledge of the employer's operations to release trade secrets or sensitive information. In the business world, trade secrets and sensitive information can include customer and client lists, business practices, pending new products, and marketing plans. Pretty serious stuff!

In the NFL, the secrets and sensitive information can include intimate knowledge by the coach of his prior team's players and remaining coaches, and their tendencies, strengths and weaknesses. It includes intimate knowledge of his prior team's offensive and defensive schemes and systems, tendencies within them, as well as on-field signals, snap cadences, game plans, and playbooks. Pretty serious stuff!

In 2000, Bill Parcells, an NFL head coach with four different teams, authored a book entitled *The Final Season*, a chronicle of the 1999 season with his third

Week	Site	Opponent	Line	PF	PA	SU	ATS	Assistant from Opponent
1	*h*	*Atlanta*	–2	13	27	L	L	*None*
2	at	NY Giants	+10	35	32	W	W	Sean Payton, OC 2000–'02
3		Bye						
4	at	NY Jets	+3	17	6	W	W	Maurice Carthon, RBs, 1997–2000
5	h	Arizona	–8	24	7	W	W	George Warhop, OL, 1998–2002
6	h	Philadelphia	+1	23	21	W	W	Sean Payton, QBs, 1997–'98
7	at	Detroit	–3	38	7	W	W	Maurice Carthon, OC, 2001–'02
8	*at*	*Tampa Bay*	+6	0	16	L	L	*None*

FIGURE 16-1 *Dallas Cowboys, 2003*

and supposedly final team, the New York Jets. "I wish my final season could have been better," he wrote at the end of the book, "but there's no shame in leaving when you know for sure it's time to go." Then, in 2003, Parcells knew for sure that it was time to come back, this time as head coach of the Dallas Cowboys. The media blew the trumpets, hailed his re-arrival and wondered how long it would take for him to engineer a turnaround from three consecutive 5-11 SU seasons by Dallas, four straight losing seasons overall. Away from the fanfare, Parcells quietly worked around non-compete clauses or took advantage of their absence. He stocked his first-season Dallas coaching staff with "moles"—assistants who had been embedded for significant durations in the very recent past with opponents on the upcoming schedule.

The first eight games of Parcells's comeback season with Dallas were bookended by two-score losses against opponents that Parcells had not mined for brain-picking assistance (see Figure 16-1). But look at Weeks 2 through 7 in between: 5-0 SU, 5-0 ATS for Dallas, when Dallas could boast of a trusty assistant who had been sleeping with the enemy. Trips to New York on consecutive weeks to play the Giants and Jets were made with Sean Payton, freshly removed as Giants offensive coordinator, at Parcells's side as assistant head coach, and Maurice Carthon, ex-Jets running backs coach for four years, as his offensive coordinator. In his final season with the Giants, Payton had been publicly embarrassed by

New York head coach Jim Fassel when, after several poor showings by the Giants' offense (which coincided with the death of Payton's mother), Payton was relieved of his role as play-caller by Fassel himself.

You can just imagine how the telephone conversation began. "Hello, Sean? Bill Parcells here. As you know, we'll be playing the Giants twice . . ." Payton stood right next to Parcells on the sideline for the entire game, which Dallas never trailed despite being +10.5 underdogs, with a cold, straight-ahead stare at the proceedings on the field, the most locked-in individual on Earth that night. On the other sideline, Fassel squirmed. What else could he do?

For a visit by Arizona in Week 3, Parcells's new offensive line coach George Warhop could supply plenty of info on how to handle things in both trenches because Warhop had been Cardinals' offensive line coach for the prior four seasons. A visit by Philadelphia the following week was eased once again by the presence of Payton, who had game-planned against the Eagles at least twice in each of the four prior seasons with New York, and who had come to the Giants from the Eagles' staff. The next game at Detroit was facilitated by having Carthon on hand, who, between his jobs with the Jets and Cowboys, had been Lions' offensive coordinator for two seasons.

Before the five-game, mole-aided streak started, Dallas had looked bad against Atlanta and a backup quarterback on their own home field on Opening Day. No member of the 2003 Dallas coaching staff had been associated with Atlanta in recent seasons. The streak would end in Tampa Bay, another place where no member of the 2003 Dallas staff had been on the payroll. Neither Atlanta (5-11) nor Tampa Bay (7-9) was good that season. In between, there were two outright Dallas wins as road underdogs, comfortable wins and covers when favored, and the end to the franchise's most embarrassing losing streak-eight games over four seasons vs. Philadelphia. Pretty serious stuff! But the most impressive item for our point-spread purposes was the 5-0 ATS.

Parity of talent among NFL teams opens the door for generally unseen factors like professional coaching network experience, knowledge and application to represent a significant edge for one team against another. Not only does the NFL wagerer need to know his coordinators and how they prefer to utilize their talent within their preferred systems, but the NFL wagerer needs to know the network. Where have these coaches been? What might they know? Who do they know? Who have they worked with in the past? Have they successfully game-planned against this opponent with another team in the past?

The more recent the switch, the better the chances of a coach (or, coaches) to pull a fast one against their ex-team, which normally will be maintaining enough personnel, coaches, systems, and schemes for the ex-coaches to maneuver around adeptly, given a competent team to work with. Rarely, if ever, is greater-than-normal coaching intimacy with the opponent built into the point-spread. But as the Dallas example displays, it can help put a big gap between a team and the spread when the game is over.

Payton is a terrific example of how tracing and locating connections in the NFL coaching web, and correctly anticipating their degree of potential impact, creates strings of targeted opportunities to help produce dividends for the patiently productive NFL wagerer. Payton was a Dallas assistant under Parcells for three seasons before making a vertical move to become head coach of the New Orleans Saints in 2006. In Week 14 of that season, New Orleans traveled to Dallas. Hey, if it was going to be circled on Sean Payton's calendar, it sure as heck was going to be circled on *Sports Reporter's*!

Best Bet

NEW ORLEANS (+6.5) over DALLAS

". . . A big key here is that the Cowboys are being targeted by men who until recently got their paychecks signed by Cowboys' owner Jerry Jones. The New Orleans game-planning here is being done by head coach Sean Payton—Cowboys' ex-offensive coordinator and assistant head coach who currently calls the offensive plays for the Saints—and Gary Gibbs, the Saints' defensive coordinator who was Dallas linebackers coach under Bill Parcells from 2002–05 . . . Does New Orleans have the defensive personnel to hold down Dallas's myriad of offensive weapons? On the surface, no. But if any opponent can draw up schemes to at least limit the Romo machine and exploit the Dallas defense, New Orleans appears to have some qualified guys."

The final score was 42-17 for New Orleans, but it was 21-7 at halftime, and 42-17 after three quarters. The destruction was swift, sudden, and decisive, punctuated by 3 touchdowns from the Saints' little-used fullback Mike Karney, who summarized the event very nicely. "He [Payton] knew them like a book." Saints quarterback Drew Brees of his head coach, "Being [in Dallas] for three years, he knew a lot of the personnel. 'This route works better against this guy or this guy . . .'"

It isn't necessary for the point-spread player, to know the exact details of what coaches may know intimately about an opponent they once worked for. Just being aware of the network is key, to be on alert for uncommonly strong exploitable opportunities. Also, be aware that what goes around comes around. As mentioned in an earlier chapter, Payton and the Saints were victimized the very same way the very next season. As –13 favorites, the New Orleans offense was successfully harassed and exploited by the man that Payton replaced as head coach in New Orleans, St. Louis Rams' defensive coordinator Jim Haslett.

Jim Fassel, fired by the Giants after that 2003 season, was sitting in the payback seat against them in December, 2004 after he had taken a step down to be an offensive assistant with Baltimore. The Ravens, losers of two straight games yet favored by −10 points against the Giants, produced their biggest points total of the season in a 37-14 win. They couldn't have made the line high enough to sway us. Baltimore was a *Sports Reporter* Super Best Bet!

Was it a coincidence that Baltimore head coach Brian Billick hired Fassel prior to a season when Baltimore would be pitted against the four NFC East teams that Fassel's Giants had played twice a year during his seven-year tenure? Probably not. Was it a coincidence that Baltimore went 4-0 ATS against New York, Dallas, Washington, and Philadelphia? Probably not. Smart general managers and coaches hire credentials. It's not always who they know. What the candidate knows—and the timeliness of it—is important. In 2007, when Ken Whisenhunt made a vertical move to Arizona head coach from Pittsburgh offensive coordinator, it coincided with Arizona's four games against AFC North opponents, the division rivals that Pittsburgh had faced twice a year. Whisenhunt brought an ex-Pittsburgh assistant to Arizona with him, offensive line coach Russ Grimm. Arizona beat the Steelers outright as +5.5 underdogs, and went 3-1 SU 4-0 ATS against the AFC North in 2007.

Before the 2004 season, the Steelers hired a new defensive coordinator. Dick LeBeau was only one season removed from having been the Cincinnati Bengals head coach, a post from which he had been fired. The Steelers proceeded to go 2-0 SU and ATS against the Bengals and advanced to the 2004 AFC Championship Game. In 2005, the Steelers won two out of three against Cincinnati, knocking them out of the playoffs on the Bengals' home field. The web extending through the Pittsburgh defensive coordinator position reached all the way to New York in December when Tim Lewis—who had been fired by the Steelers and replaced by LeBeau—was preparing the Giants' defensive unit for a home game against the Steelers. The Steelers entered the game after allowing only 29 points combined in their previous three games. Was it a coincidence that in that game the Giants—a 6-10 team in 2004—scored the most regular season points (30) against Pittsburgh when the Steelers' ex-defensive coordinator was calling the shots against them for New York? Probably not. It was an easy cover for home underdog New York at +10, the very next game after the Giants had been mercilessly exploited by their own ex-coach Fassel at Baltimore!

Warning! Targeting and capitalizing on these recurring situations could cause you to get carried away and see connections that exist, but a little too loosely, and lack the dynamic potential to affect the outcome. I have learned that lesson the hard way. Bad teams normally do not have the talent to respond to the coaching intimacy edge, and the very good teams will often have the talent to overcome these potential traps against them. For instance, there was 2006 Week 5 with the Buffalo Bills, +10 at Chicago. Thinking that all I needed was four recent ex-Bears in the Buffalo meeting room to negotiate around the land mines against a strong, Super Bowl-bound Bears team gave new meaning to the term "fantasy" football. Dick Jauron, fired as head coach in Chicago and replaced with Lovie Smith, was the first-season Buffalo head coach and had plucked two of his Bills' assistants from the Bears' staff. Marv Levy, last year's Bears radio analyst, was now the Buffalo team president. That was the most comical gaffe, expecting an 81-year-old radio analyst hired as a feel-good figurehead (Levy had coached Buffalo to four Super Bowl appearances) to provide think-tank contributions with ex-Bears coaches who were coaching a bad Buffalo team. The reality of the situation was that a young, inexperienced, turnover-prone Buffalo quarterback (J.P. Losman) would be facing the most turnover-crazed defense in the NFL. This was a Best Bet that exploded worse than an ACME device on Wile E. Coyote when Losman threw 3 interceptions, while the Bills' offense lost 2 fumbles and had a punt blocked. The mistakes made by Buffalo were all very predictable, yet all very ignored by me in an attempt to uncover a hidden jewel.

I made a big turnover by forcing a frequently productive play into coverage, even though I was well aware that the coverage existed. Hey, it happens, especially when you allow yourself to get overconfident from past successes won by making correct connections. As long as you admit to the mistake, feel the hurt and learn from it, you minimize the chances of it happening again.

Every NFL team web site at nfl.com contains biographies about the head coach and assistants for that season, including previous teams, tenures, and posts held. If you Google an NFL head coach, coordinator or assistant, chances are that a link containing his bio will be returned among the top searches. If not, a search for it at Wikipedia.com, the online encyclopedia, is almost a guarantee to produce a complete background on your head coach or coordinator. All the information is out there at everyone's fingertips. There is no excuse for not knowing the network.

17
Totals: The Universe is Out of Alignment!

MANY BETTORS WILL bankrupt themselves betting against what is happening over and over again when what they call a "due theory" is merely a guess with absolutely no substance to it. But Bill Gates, the Microsoft king, has issued the tools to refine sports projection approaches to the point where a certain type of "due theory" is very, very valid, yet very, very under-the-radar. Bill Gates has empowered me, and all other PC users, with the resources to look beyond the obvious to see future results to which others are still blind.

The Microsoft Office software program is to NFL investors what Queen Isabella was to Columbus, and what improvements in telescope lenses were to Copernicus and Galileo. Within Microsoft Office, the Microsoft Excel and Microsoft Access applications combine to form the single-most powerful forecasting tool, used to predict with the most confidence, results that represent a dramatic change from generally accepted current trends.

Copernicus and Galileo were maverick geniuses because they used the tools at hand to make discoveries of their own, while the rest of their countrymen were too stubborn to entertain ideas and practices outside of their own defunct worldview. It's this ability to utilize the tools of the day and make progress that separates a great man from the rest of the herd, and a good ATS man from a sucker.

The NFL Totals Universe

Before the 2006 season began, NFL Totals Universe was arranged in a relatively neat high-low plot. The "Total Margin" is the per game average of the winning and losing score, minus the Wagering Total. For instance, if the Wagering Total

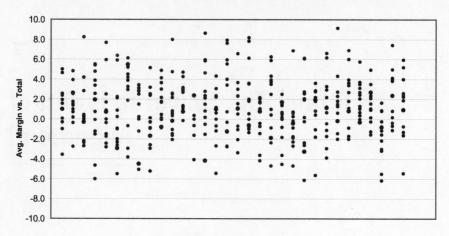

FIGURE 17-1 1993–2005

for Indianapolis at Denver is 41, a final score of 34-31 earns each side a Total Margin of +24 for the game.

The most "Over" that any team had played during the course of a 16-game regular season was Indianapolis, +8.6 vs. the Total in 2001. The most Under that any team had played for a season in the same span was Carolina, –7.4 in 2000. As you can see, the vast majority of seasonal Total Margins are clustered between +4.0 and –4.0. "Outer limits" teams like extremely low-score Carolina in '00, and extremely high-score Indianapolis in '01, were the exceptions that framed the rest of the NFL Totals Universe.

NFL Totals Sky

Which doesn't belong and why? That's a relatively easy one, isn't it? On the eve of NFL Week 8, anyone gazing into their NFL Totals telescope saw a rare celestial phenomenon. One of bodies in orbit—the Denver Broncos—experienced logging results that defied the gravitational forces of the NFL Universe. By averaging almost –17 points below the Wagering Total, Denver games were way outside the orbit range of NFL planets. The average Denver game was going Under by two touchdowns and a field goal!

The '06 Broncos had played nothing but Unders to this point, their six games having landed Under the total in a range from –7 to –24.5 points. To the untrained eye, Denver was not coming back to the pack because there was no pack to see. Denver was simply "6-0 to the Under."

Without a telescope to look at our night skies, the planet Saturn looks like any other ordinary star. But with the aid of a simple telescope, its rings are clearly visible. Without a telescope, Venus looks like a bright star. But with the aid of

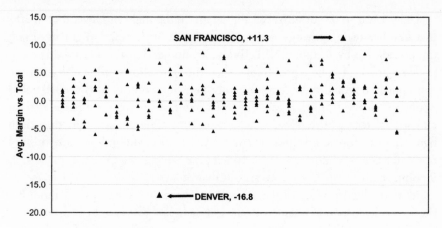

FIGURE 17-2 Saturday, November 4, 2006

a simple telescope, its crescent image is clearly visible. Without a telescope, the planet Jupiter looks like an ordinary star. But with the aid of a simple telescope, not only is Jupiter distinguished from stars with odd coloring, but six otherwise invisible moons clearly appear around the mother planet.

To anyone without superior knowledge of the high and low vertical limits of the NFL Totals Universe, the Denver Broncos' "6-0 Under" looked like just another trend that it would be foolish to oppose in their next game. But the laws of NFL Totals have clearly demonstrated to be more powerful than any one team that happened to be in orbit a season as far from the full season cluster as Denver was. With the '00 Carolina Panthers (–7.4) as the nearest outpost, the Broncos were playing more than twice as Under after six games as any NFL team in their generation had for a full season.

Their next Denver opponent was the Indianapolis Colts, quarterbacked by the era's best at the position, Peyton Manning. To that point in the 2006 season, the average Colts' game score was 28.5 to 20.3, and average of 49 points. For the three prior seasons, Colts games points totals had averaged 49, 52.5 and 43 points. The Wagering Total for this game was only 39.

To make a long story short, the final score in Indianapolis at Denver that day was 34-31.

In exceeding the Total by +26 points, the result jolted Denver's Total Margin down to –10.6. By season's end eight weeks later, Denver's final 2006 Total Margin was all the way on the other side of zero at +2.1, in the cluster with 95 percent of the other NFL teams of its generation. Their orbit had been headed there all along, and a meeting with the Colts was the perfect time for the ship to be caught by the gravitational pull of the other planets and make a sharp turn back towards the center of the universe.

Denver was so out of universal alignment on the night of November 4, 2006 that another team existing outside the accepted orbit range might have gone unnoticed even by an expert NFL Totals astronomer. But the 49ers didn't escape my view at +11.4, a field goal higher than the generation's full season high. But San Francisco would be playing the unbeaten Bears on the road the next afternoon, a Chicago team that was making a habit of scoring on offense, defense, and special teams. The 49ers' course would certainly change. But they didn't figure to be re-routed on this particular day. The Bears did indeed score multiple non-offensive touchdowns in a 41-10 win, the game going Over a Total of 42 by 9 points, close to the Niners' average at that point.

In a Straight-Up recap of the 49ers-Bears game, the writer mused about how the 49ers' defense was extremely poor, and on a pace to allow the most points in an NFL season. This inaccurate observation disregarded how the San Francisco defense had merely been set up to fail by turnovers made by the offense, and unfairly credited the 49ers' defense with allowing opposing special teams touchdowns. The scoreboard had shown that San Francisco's "defense" had given up 34 to 48 points in five of its seven games, and the Wagering Total for their next game was "only" 42.

San Francisco's next opponent was Minnesota, a home-dome team playing outdoors on grass that was averaging only 15 first downs per game and had injuries on its offensive line. The Vikings' defense was hanging in there, allowing more than 19 points only once in seven previous games. San Francisco's offensive coordinator Norv Turner had once been the head coach for Minnesota's quarterback, Brad Johnson. Turner knew as well as anyone how a defense could bring the worst out of Johnson. While the naked eyes were expecting a high-scoring affair and San Francisco's seventh Over in eight games, I had other ideas after viewing the NFL Totals Sky: "BEST BET TOTAL—UNDER 42, MINNESOTA at SAN FRANCISCO."

The final score was 9-3.

By falling 30 points shy of the Total in this game, the 49ers' Total Margin for the season dropped sharply, to a level within the pre-established full season borders. By the end of the 2006 season, San Francisco would be re-routed in the opposite direction of where they had been, just as Denver had been. After playing six Overs in the first seven games, the 49ers played six Unders in the last nine games. Their full season margin of –2.7 vs. the Total landed San Francisco on the opposite side of zero from where their orbit had been plotted after eight weeks. When all was said and done, the 49ers were just another spot in the vast cluster, as they and the majority of NFL teams are meant to be within the great NFL Totals Universe.

. . .

My FIRST STAR-GAZING experience with NFL Totals was in the 2003 season, while in search of ways to disprove and downgrade simple, weighted ATS records as a meaningful projection tool. It happened while tinkering with historical NFL result data in a Microsoft Excel spreadsheet, information that included point-spreads and totals for every game. After reading what I thought was yet another in a long line of useless articles about an NFL player on pace to break a "record," I got to thinking about how nobody out there in ATS World had ever tracked and published record highs and lows in our parallel world—at least, not publicly.

Most readers of this book know someone who qualifies as an intermediate Excel and Access user and would know how to link Excel data to Access, then write some very simple template-driven queries to analyze the continuous com-pilation of plain old results.

Luckily for me at the time, I was one of those Excel and Access intermediate level users. Almost as instantly and accidentally as Charles Goodyear had discov-ered vulcanized rubber, I discovered an NFL Totals Universe. Compared to every other team within that universe, the Cleveland Browns were in a very odd place.

NFL Totals Sky

Saturday, November 1, 2003

The Browns, at −11.4 points per game Under the Total to that point, were the only 2003 team not playing within the already established high and low vs. the Total. They would have a bye the next day, but the Browns were scheduled to play at Kansas City the following Sunday. Chiefs games had averaged 54 total points the prior season and were averaging 49 to that point in the season. The Cleveland at Kansas City Wagering Total was 44.

The final score was 41-20. Chiefs.

Going Over the Total by three scores dragged the Browns back toward the cluster, but they were still beyond 2000 Carolina at −8.11. However, Cleveland's rightful place in the universe was soon "fixed." In the very next game, the Browns scored a season-high 44 points in a game that went Over the total by 12 points. Now at −6.1 points vs. the Total after 10 games, they were on the fringes of the Under-world, but within the range of pre-established orbits within the NFL Totals Universe.

The opportunity to capitalize on a messed up NFL Totals Sky that is due to straighten itself out is pretty much an annual phenomenon presenting itself somewhere in a range spanning early to mid-October through mid-December. Hey, it's shorter than the annual hurricane season in the U.S., with more predict-able results!

• • •

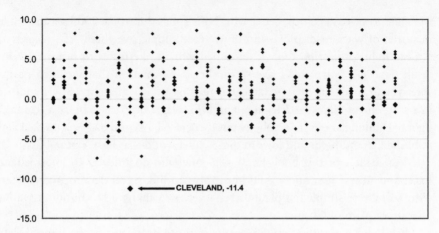

FIGURE 17-3 NFL Totals Sky

NFL Totals Skies

2006: Sunday, December 16
San Diego Chargers: +13.2 vs. Total

Chargers games had been lighting up scoreboards. Eight of their last nine games had gone Over the Total. But San Diego was pitched in an orbit more than 60 percent farther away from the pre-established outer limit. They were next playing Kansas City, whose coaches were in the process of implementing a new, defensive-minded philosophy. Also, head coach Herman Edwards and defensive coordinator Gunther Cunningham had each worked as assistants on other NFL staffs under San Diego head coach Marty Schottenheimer. Edwards and Cunningham would be employing a tricky Cover-2 defense against first-season NFL starting quarterback Philip Rivers, inviting San Diego to throw into a trap, fully aware that Schottenheimer would choose to run, run, run instead. Against a Wagering Total of 46.5, the final score was 20-9.

2007: Sunday, November 12

Miami Dolphins: +20.2 vs. Total

Two weeks before this game, I e-mailed this message to a networker, giving him some advance notice: "Miami is playing at +20.2 vs. the total. "I will target 'Under of the Year #2' when Miami hits Philadelphia in Week 11, to lose 20-6 at a line of 44."

Actually, the eventual result was 17-7 at a line of 40.5. Pretty sharp, eh? But I'm not smart enough to be able to see this on my own. Without assistance from the tools that expose the NFL Totals Universe, opportunities like these would fly by unseen.

2007: Saturday, December 8

Cleveland Browns: +11.42 vs. Total
New England Patriots: +11.25 vs. Total

This was classic beauty. Like when Venus and the moon are twinkling together in a crisp, clear winter sky. New England and Cleveland were each 9-2-1 Over/Under/Tie to that point. But, as noted by their Total Margins above, their orbits were too far out for this late in the season. On Sunday, December 9, their results eked Under the Total by –1 point, and –5.5 points—relative slivers compared to the above standout opportunities. But winners nevertheless on the "under due" notice served, with neither result pulling them back far enough to rejoin the rest of the planets in the NFL Totals Universe. After playing 13 games of their 16 games, New England was still at +10.2, Cleveland at +10.1. The real payoff was about to take place. The opening lines for their next games looked like this:

NY Jets at New England: 46
Buffalo at Cleveland: 43

The weather forecast for each venue was colder than normal, windier than normal, with some precipitation. By game time, the Totals for each game were driven downward to levels that the offenses of both New England and Cleveland had individually eclipsed on their own several times apiece during the season:

NY Jets at New England: 41
Buffalo at Cleveland: 36

Yet there was still plenty of value to be gained by projecting a final score below those numbers, as you can see by the actual results that yielded Under winners by two and four scores:

New England, 20-10
Cleveland, 8-0

Gravity, baby. You don't mess with, or doubt, the power of Mother Nature. You do your best to stay in tune with it, anticipate the flow, and roll with it. NFL team scores always seek their level vs. the Wagering Total as a season progresses. The two highest-scoring NFL teams of all time both played Unders in the Super Bowl. You have seen a working forecasting model that adds detail, dimension, and direction to otherwise flat, static results. The use of simple, alternative math uncovers a result's destiny before it happens, year, after year, after year.

If you think that NFL Totals Universe gazing is too complicated to perform on your own, please think again. I flunked both geometry and statistics in high school and earned Cs in college-level math. Computer classes? Forget about it. The user-friendly world created by Bill Gates and Microsoft programmers is your ticket to the "edge" of the Universe. This particular method of analyzing and capitalizing on NFL totals is very similar to timing the stock market. Promotional text for *The Streetsmart Guide to Timing the Stock Market* says,

> *Market timing is one of the most enticing yet hard-to-grasp tools for active traders looking to beat competing traders and the overall market . . . reveals how recent market developments can help you spot pending turnarounds, detailing short trading opportunities as well as warning signs of a short trade about to turn bad.*

They say that it is every investor's dream to time the stock market, because a successful market timer does not have to possess any real stock-picking skills. Well, if you want to turn a dream into reality, look up at the NFL Totals Sky every late autumn and you'll see some twinkling opportunities that you have the power to make come true without having to wish for them.

18
Weather and Surface

NOBODY—NOT ONE SINGLE person with either cable television, or computer and Internet access—ever has the excuse of being surprised by rain, snow, or windy weather affecting a game in which they have a vested interest in a side or total. If the game is being played outdoors, and you plan on being on it, then it is your responsibility to know what the likely conditions will be. You can bet your butt that the coaches have checked the advance forecast at *www.weather.com* or the Weather Channel before creating their game plans, to make sure they don't show up with a plan to pass all afternoon in driving wind and rain. It is also your responsibility to know which stadiums have domes, because domes eliminate weather from the equation. When bad weather is a threat, the retractable domes will be closed, removing that threat. But some retractable-dome stadiums house natural grass surfaces, unlike the strictly-artificial surfaces that were standard-issue in older domed stadiums.

The author of this book got a little overzealous in a college football forecast once, saw windy snowstorms forecast in Moscow, Idaho for Saturday afternoon at kickoff time, and blasted an "Under" forecast in *Sports Reporter* for a Sun Belt Conference game based on two passing teams being hampered by the bad weather conditions. The name of the stadium where the University of Idaho plays football? The Kibbie Dome. As the snow swirled outside, everyone inside was quite comfy, especially the offenses playing to a final score of 35-31.

That is the kind of mistake you make only once.

In most instances, extraordinarily poor weather—if it exists—and the surface—which always exists—are not the highest-priority factors in the final equation. They are common-sense factors that need to be known along with as many other seen and unseen match-up factors, and assessed for their potential to either create an advantage for one side or the other, or to affect the total of points scored in the game. After all, one of the biggest myths in the NFL is the "Frozen Tundra of Lambeau Field" in Green Bay, where heating pipes keep the playing surface heated to about 50 degrees during games in cold weather. From 1993 to 2007, Packers home games in December and January had an Over-Under split of 25-19, 57 percent Over, which runs contrary to conventional wisdom. But you have to remember that conventional wisdom and common sense are two different things. Conventional wisdom is people doubting that either the Giants or Packers could score points in the 2007 NFC Championship Game, played at night in late January, with the temperature at 1 degree and the wind chill making it feel even colder. Well, they combined for 43 points on the way to exceeding the Total of 40.5. Common sense is in knowing that the field ain't frozen and never will be. Conventional wisdom also says, "The Packers play in cold weather, so they will probably cover the spread when it's cold and they are home." They happen to have been 13-10 ATS in Green Bay in December and January from 1993 to 2007, for anyone out there who might have been working on a 15-year plan involving 23 games. "Green Bay in the cold," is mostly a legendary thing, trotted out to hype the moment when necessary. When Green Bay (−7) stood 7-1 ATS for the 2007 season at Lambeau Field and went out to play for the NFC Championship Game in 1-degree weather on a 50-degree home field, reality beat legend when the New York Giants outplayed the Packers up and down that field.

The overall home-field records in Table 19-1 can be misleading. Buffalo, a team in a cold-weather city, has the best home ATS record among Northern teams. But in December and January home games from 2000 through 2007, the Bills were just 9-9 ATS. Jacksonville, a warm-weather Florida team with the NFL's best overall home record vs. the spread, was 8-4 ATS in September home games in that span. But guess what? Before 2007, when their reputation may not have preceded them in bettors' minds, that home-field ATS record in September was 8-2 ATS. When friendly confines and customary weather are prevalent, they can erase the fact that the line and the match-up still matter. In September '07, the Jags were asked to cover two scores in their September home games, with a new starting quarterback. One of the games was against home-dome visitor Atlanta, playing outdoors on grass in 88-degree temps, and 81 percent humidity. But the Jags didn't get it done for their "trend" players either time.

Beyond plain hot and cold, more severe weather is still easier to predict accurately than the outcome of an NFL game, because meteorologists can actually see frontal systems moving and have instruments that measure the elements within them, like barometric pressure and wind speed. (Bettors have instruments to measure systems, too, as you have been reminded of at various points throughout the book.) Weather Channel information at www.weather.com is narrowed down to forecasting conditions at given time intervals during the day, several days in advance. Therefore, when you see, 48 hours in advance, "40 mph

Home ATS, 1993–2007	W	L	T	ATS%
Jacksonville	60	43	4	58.3%
Baltimore	54	40	5	57.4%
Dallas	66	52	10	55.9%
Kansas City	65	52	7	55.6%
Buffalo	66	54	4	55.0%
Pittsburgh	72	59	2	55.0%
Houston	25	21	2	54.3%
Green Bay	65	55	10	54.2%
Tampa Bay	65	55	5	54.2%
Detroit	62	55	4	53.0%
Minnesota	64	57	4	52.9%
New England	66	59	7	52.8%
Cleveland	49	45	3	52.1%
Philadelphia	64	59	7	52.0%
Chicago	62	58	5	51.7%
San Francisco	62	60	7	50.8%
Carolina	52	51	3	50.5%
Denver	62	61	3	50.4%
NY Giants	60	62	3	49.2%
Tennessee	60	62	2	49.2%
Arizona	58	60	2	49.2%
San Diego	58	63	4	47.9%
Seattle	58	65	3	47.2%
Miami	56	63	5	47.1%
NY Jets	54	63	5	46.2%
Indianapolis	57	67	3	46.0%
Atlanta	54	64	4	45.8%
Cincinnati	52	66	3	44.1%
Washington	51	65	5	44.0%
St. Louis	53	68	4	43.8%
Oakland	50	71	5	41.3%
New Orleans	47	72	3	39.5%

FIGURE 18-1

wind gusts" predicted for Chicago on a Sunday afternoon when the Bears are hosting the Packers, and the total is 42 on Friday, you are taking all the worst of it if you wait until Sunday at 12:30 pm to play the Under, when the Wagering Total has changed to 36 on Sunday morning, and 31.5 by kickoff time! In that particular instance, the margin for error was greater for Sunday bettors than for Thursday bettors, by the considerable sizes of 14.2 percent to 25 percent, depending on what time Sunday morning the wagers were made. (This is another reason for ignoring point-spread records. How is it that a win or a push for Thursday bettors and a loss for Sunday bettors is universally recorded as one specific result, yet still considered to be accurate?)

Because of reactionary changes in the Total line, and because football is harder to predict than weather, there is no guarantee of being rewarded for acting "the right way" upon your weather research. No Under players won the Green Bay at Chicago game. Some people who wagered on it to go Under were surpassed by the Bears alone in Chicago's 35-7 win. The weather conditions were truly difficult, including 16 degrees, swirling winds gusting to 40 mph, and some snow. Packers' quarterback Brett Favre called it the worst conditions he had ever played in during his 17 seasons in the NFL. Each offense gained only about 270 yards. But the Bears returned a blocked punt and an interception for touchdowns, and they were set up for cheap, short-drive offensive scores by another punt block and interception. These things happen. But at the same time, that particular Bears team was known for scoring points on special teams and defense. Therefore, nobody who factored the weather into their Under gets a free pass for making that incorrect determination.

Coincidentally, another Green Bay vs. Chicago game, played on Halloween night of the 1996 season, is further evidence of reasonable reaction to weather that doesn't quite work out. The Monday Night game—which opened at a total of 41.5 and was bet down to 34 by game-time—was played in a steady downpour with 30 mph winds and temperatures in the 30s, on soggy grass at Soldier Field. A younger Favre and the Packers came into Soldier Field averaging 33.4 points per game, to Chicago's 15.0. Bears starting quarterback Eric Kramer reportedly told the offensive coordinator, "Don't call a pass, I can't throw anything." The score was 0-0 at the end of the first quarter, when Green Bay punted four times into the wind. The Bears' offense could not move the ball. At that point, the Under looked solid at both the high opening and low closing ends of the established range. But then the Packers, on their way to 223 rushing yards and 5 turnovers acquired from the Bears, scored on 2 touchdown drives with the wind at their backs in the second quarter for a 14-0 halftime lead. The Packers opened the second half with the football and the wind, and off a Bears fumble and a short Bears punt against the stiff wind, scored 2 more touchdowns on short drives. The garbage time score was 33-0 as the clock mercifully ticked down. On a desperate, hurry-up offensive series, the Bears scored a "meaningless" late touchdown to make it 33-6. "He goes 'Over' the goal line," said play-by-play announcer Al Michaels, for whom the number 34 apparently had special meaning.

That's football, that's line movement, and, with the Packers averaging 33.4 points per game coming in, that's what can happen when weather helps spring a flood of turnovers and one of the teams (in this case, Chicago) doesn't have a good defense. Foul weather can assist Unders, but they can also help kill them after the number comes down and the turnover count they help produce goes up. It can also beat them if a passing team—like Green Bay was with Favre at quarterback—throws more incompletions than usual to stop the clock and lengthen the game via more plays within the 60-minute time frame. It is better to have already liked a game to go Under before the bad weather is factored, than to make bad weather the sole factor for an Under selection.

• • •

NFL TEAMS THAT play their games in domed stadiums on artificial turf tend to be built for speed and points. There can be exceptions, but it's also no surprise that the 2007 New England Patriots set numerous offensive records that had previously been set by St. Louis and Minnesota in the 1990s as home-dome teams that played on artificial turf. When weather will never be a factor, it makes perfect sense for a general manager to gear his team towards becoming a big-play, upper-echelon passing offense matched with a quick, opportunistic, big-play defense. Most visiting opponents who play outdoors—especially opponents located in cold-weather cities—will be geared down by comparison. In a league whose rules have been shifted to favor offense over defense, it makes even more sense to construct a domed home team in that manner.

Do big scores translate to automatic Overs? No way, Jose. The lines for domed teams account for the average points scored and allowed in the past both home and away, and the numbers they are asked to clear are usually higher, on average, than for teams that play outdoors on grass. Everything is relative.

From 2000 though 2007, the average game totals for St. Louis and Indianapolis indoor-turf home games were 46.5 and 46.1, the two highest in the NFL. During the same span, the average total for Baltimore and Tampa Bay home games was 36.7 and 37.3, the two lowest in the NFL. Even as defensive-minded Baltimore shifted from natural grass to artificial turf, their personnel remained essentially the same and their offense was not in position to respond favorably to the change. The median average team total in that span was 41.0, and all six indoor home-dome turf teams were on the high side of that median. But the Over-Under results for the home games of the six indoor-turf teams in that span were 201-196. The 50.6 percent Over rate would have represented a flat-bet net loss on Over. The year the Colts became just the second home-dome team to win the Super Bowl, their 10 home games (including post-season) had a 5-5 Over/Under split despite their status as the second-highest scoring team in the AFC. One season earlier, when the Colts made it as far as the AFC Championship Game, their games resulted in just 2-7 Over-Under despite their status as the highest-scoring team in the AFC. Many opposing head coaches, like Tennessee's Jeff Fisher, tried to bully the Colts by running the ball and eating the clock in an attempt to keep the ball out of the hands of MVP quarterback Peyton Manning. It was the ol' "stay in it with a chance to win it late" plan. "They are not equipped to stop the run for four quarters," said Fisher. "That's the way they are built." However, that particular strategy was essentially a "pick your poison" move, as the Colts were actually good enough to withstand a strategy tailored especially against them and win games with lower scores than they had played to in the past. Eventually, it frustrated Fisher to the point where he changed offensive coordinators in an attempt to ramp up his team's ability to put points on the board instead of just milking the clock and punting.

When the six dome teams played each other from 2000 to 2007, the Totals result was 43-41, another net loss on Over at 51.1 percent. On outdoor fields during those eight years, the Over-Under split was 820-895, 52.2 percent Under.

· · ·

ON NOVEMBER 12, 2006 the New England Patriots lost 17-14 to the New York Jets on a rain-slicked, chopped up grass field. It was New England's fifth home game of the season. All five landed Under the total. The next Patriots home game was two weeks away, and it would be played on a new artificial surface called FieldTurf, which would be in place at nine NFL stadiums as of the 2007 season. The debut of the new field late in the season, against the rock-solid defense and sorry offense of the Chicago Bears, resulted in a 17-13 final score that was Under the total. But after the Chicago game, the next three Patriots home games—all played in December and January—would go Over the total by a touchdown or more. In 2007, the first five Patriots home games went Over the total, for a stretch of eight consecutive Overs on the heels of six consecutive Unders. Under in Patriots home games on the grass at Gillette Stadium had actually been the norm for four seasons beginning in 2003: The Over/Under Ratios in Foxborough from 2003 to 2006 were 3-7, 3-6, 3-6, and 3-6, for 12-25, which was 67.5 percent Under.

Was it a coincidence that the streak of eight straight Overs began shortly after the surface switch from natural grass to artificial turf? Or, was the streak the result of cause-and-effect? It was probably the latter. Between the 2006 and 2007 seasons, the Patriots—whose defense was older than average—made an obvious effort towards tailoring their team to the new home surface and its penchant for assisting offensive playmakers via consistently-surer footing. They acquired top-echelon deep-threat wide receivers Randy Moss and Donte Stallworth, plus possession receiver Wes Welker. Three- and four-wide receiver alignments that the Patriots had tinkered with in 2006 became somewhat standard in 2007, and the team set numerous NFL offensive records.

Was it a coincidence that the 2003 New York Giants went 1-7 ATS on their home field in the first year of a switch from natural grass to FieldTurf? Probably not. A relatively slow, veteran defense suffered more injuries and yielded 24.7 points per game after allowing only 18.7 in 2002. As mentioned in a previous chapter, was it a coincidence that Miami and Pittsburgh played the lowest scoring NFL game in 14 years immediately after the Steelers' Heinz Field was re-sodded and the game played in the rain? Probably not. The 3-0 final occurred as Pittsburgh was averaging 26 points per game, and Miami's opponents were scoring 29 points per game.

The message here, once again, is to always be on alert for changes that fly under the public radar. You want to be the guy who spots them, makes a logical connection to their pending impact, and immediately makes repeated successful moves that fly in the face of the established status quo.

19
Money Management
_____

FOR AN INDIVIDUAL working the NFL point-spread arena independently or with a group, consider any money management plan to be suspect if it involves anything beyond sticking to straight wagers at the same amount per side or total. Anyone with the discipline to stick to wagering the same amount on every selection for an entire season will have netted a serious accomplishment in itself, and is then eligible to experiment with finding a better way. Chances are they won't find it.

Part of the problem that I have with most attempts at laying out a money management plan is that no matter what size bankroll is established at the beginning, there is no accurate way to measure and allocate its distribution against the number of games you might eventually be playing, or the sequence of wins and losses. Let's get one thing straight. Choosing to bet on a set number of games per week is definitely not part of a sound money management plan. You are holding the trigger, therefore, you wager when you are confident that a targeted opportunity is in your crosshairs. You do not fire indiscriminately just because you like to hear the bang. Odds are pretty safe that nobody is holding a gun to your head to wager on a set number of games. If somebody is, then you must wrestle that gun away from him, point it at his head, and say, "How do *you* like being forced to wager instead of being able to pick and choose your spots, eh, buddy!?"

First of all, let's establish generally-expected rates of return from some other forms of investing as we sit here in the early stages of the new millennium:

In February 2008, *Money* magazine published its list of "The Best Mutual Funds You Can Buy." Among the 42 actively-managed funds listed, the most recent one-year return rates ranged from −29.2 percent up to 24.2 percent, and 69 percent of the funds showed a loss for the last year. None of the yields shown in Figure 19-1 are outstanding in their own right. But let's not kid ourselves. Smart investing is usually a slow and steady way to make a profit. NFL betting is a four-month series of high-risk ventures. For instance,

Sports Reporter published "NFL Best Bets" in the 2007 season were 33-21, for 61.1 percent wins. At $200 per (which would have been an outlay of $11,880), they would have netted $1,980, a return of 16.7 percent—a rate more than three times better than a typical six-month CD during approximately the same time frame. The table below displays what different won-loss results would yield over the course of a 70-wager season at two different investment levels per side or total:

Why 70 wagers? No reason, other than representing a reasonable average of four games per week, plus a couple of post-season games. If that four-game per week average was realized, it could proceed in a weekly sequence of 5-3-6-5-2-5-7-1-3-6-2-4-5-3-5-3-3. Or, it could shake out in a different distribution of wagers, and it doesn't have to be four per week. It could be three per week, or two. Or, only 10 games for the whole season! Everybody is different, and nobody really knows what the total of games will be until their season has concluded. There is no optimum amount of games to select over the course of a season. For instance, one NFL side in one game, for $10,000. That could be a season right there, regardless of the result.

I recommend that anyone who might be wagering on the NFL over the course of the season—even if it's just with mythical money as opposed to being in Las Vegas—conduct a concurrent study: Results of All Personal Wagers vs. Results of One Personal Weekly Best Bet. You might learn something along the way about what types of situations you tend to see correctly vs. what might be a fantasy or forced action. When you recognize that a particular type of situation is separating itself as being more successful than others, you might be able to spot it elsewhere and learn the value of specialization, multiplying the number of live targets while weeding out those that tend to be dead wood. Or, it could work in reverse. If the one game you thought would work above all others wins with less frequency than the rest, you might detect a faulty pattern while learning about the value of diversification.

Common money management theories, after stating the obvious but necessary, "Never wager more than you can afford to lose," have dictated this guideline: "Never risk more than 5 percent or less than 2 percent of a bankroll on any single game."

First of all, this rule has been handed down through the ages and assumes that somebody is betting with an illegal neighborhood bookmaker who does not require the bankroll on account in advance. Online wagering—with account sums established in advance—has surpassed the illegal neighborhood bookmakers. For argument's sake, let's say that somebody who lives overseas has, in fact, established a set NFL season bankroll of $7,000 in an online account. If that person intends to bet five games on the first Sunday, what is the bankroll? Is it the $7,000 start level, or the $5,250 represented by the balance after five wagers

Type	Minimum Deposit	Length	Yield
CD	$10,000	6 mo. ahead	4.9%
Money Market	$10,000	Annual	4.5%
High-Interest Savings	$100	Annual	3.0%
Bonds	$1,000	5-year avg.	1.9%
S&P Stocks	–	6 mo. past	–5.6%
NASDAQ	–	6 mo. past	–10.8%

FIGURE 19-1

of $350 apiece? Then, let's say four of five wagers lose. The bankroll becomes significantly less, which decreases the amount of the maximum bet allowed by the money management system. Why should any given side or total be worth less to a person in Week 2 than it was in Week 1? This would make no sense. On the other end of the scale, if, after a 4-1 or 5-0 day, the bankroll has exceeded $8,000, is there any reason why the next week's 5 percent single-game maximum should represent a larger sum than it did the prior week? The bettor is now exposed to a larger per unit loss on a game. Games should not gain or lose their individual value with the passage of time. Anyone who wagers $350 per game and wins, then wagers $400 per game and loses, will quickly feel like an idiot and learn this lesson the hard way. You're attempting to predict NFL results here, which is a tough enough task by itself. Anyone who seriously thinks that they can successfully predict that their winning frequency will increase in correlation to the size of their wagers is being an impudent fool. A win is a win. A loss is a loss. A winning day is a winning day. A losing day is a losing day. Act like you've been there before and stay on an even keel regardless.

One of the problems with online wagering is that only a minority percentage of a $7,000 account is being utilized per week. There could be more than $5,500 sitting around not earning interest. Is there anyone out there who really feels comfortable handing over $7,000 of their money to sit in a non-interest bearing hands of someone charging them 11/10 for every purchase? This is why living in Las Vegas and playing on the fly is a better alternative than wagering online.

In the example from Figure 19-2, with 70 selections over the course of a season, the $200 player would actually be putting $15,400 into play when all is said and done, regardless of the eventual winning percentage and profit. This is why nobody should be concerned about beating the bookmaker. When the bookmaker can turn a mere mortal's $7,000 bankroll into $15,400, he is going to win. But he isn't going to beat you if you're doing your job and picking

W	L	PCT.	$200 PER	ROI	$500 PER	ROI
50	20	71.4%	$5,600	36.4%	$14,000	36.4%
48	22	68.6%	$4,760	30.9%	$11,900	30.9%
46	24	65.7%	$3,920	25.5%	$9,800	25.5%
44	26	62.9%	$3,080	20.0%	$7,700	20.0%
42	28	60.0%	$2,240	14.5%	$5,600	14.5%
40	30	57.1%	$1,400	9.1%	$3,500	9.1%
38	32	54.3%	$560	3.6%	$1,400	3.6%
36	34	51.4%	−$280	−1.8%	−$700	−1.8%
34	36	48.6%	−$1,120	−7.3%	−$2,800	−7.3%
32	38	45.7%	−$1,960	−12.7%	−$4,900	−12.7%
30	40	42.9%	−$2,800	−18.2%	−$7,000	−18.2%
28	42	40.0%	−$3,640	−23.6%	−$9,100	−23.6%
26	44	37.1%	−$4,480	−29.1%	−$11,200	−29.1%
24	46	34.3%	−$5,320	−34.5%	−$13,300	−34.5%
22	48	31.4%	−$6,160	−40.0%	−$15,400	−40.0%
20	50	28.6%	−$7,000	−45.5%	−$17,500	−45.5%

FIGURE 19-2

enough winners. Only one person can beat you. That person is you, which is why you can't afford to play any other way but disciplined. If you wake up Sunday morning not knowing what to play, you've already failed to do your job. Theoretically, you could have or should have already been down by Friday or earlier, after going through your reads like a good quarterback who lets the game come to him. You're not going out and looking for games on Sunday morning. In fact, if you happen to like the Monday Night game, you should already be on it by Sunday morning.

Any money management plan that details strategy for 4:15 p.m. games following 1 p.m. results is also doing you no favors. Some money management plans advise betting more on the late games if you have won the 1 p.m. games. They call it "playing with house money," which is exactly what the bookmaker wants you to think. It's not house money. It's *your* money. If you play foolishly with *your* money, you will lose *your* money. You haven't researched the NFL for six months to build your anticipation skills so that you can sit around and wait for 1 p.m. results to trigger more decisions and more action at 4:15 p.m. The 1 p.m. results should have you thinking about next week already. Attempting to adjust and strategize wagers on 1 p.m. to 4:15 p.m. scenarios will have a great chance to do two things: Fail, and drive you insane.

Mickey Charles says that part of the enjoyment of NFL wagering is following the fundamental guidelines, "such as not having to watch the game on which you are betting. You do not need to wager on a 4:15 p.m. game just because it's being played. Winner at 1 p.m. does not mandate action in the afternoon, and loser does not necessitate an attempt to get even. Nor need the Monday Night event be anything more than just one more listing of something to watch instead of old movies. It's a long season! One of the most important words you will ever learn is 'pass.' The most important thing to remember is that there does not exist the obligation to make a wager if the game does not appeal to you."

One of the most idiotic money management suggestions ever presented is to treat football wagering like a mutual fund with an automatic monthly sum re-invested into the bankroll—an attempt at simulating dollar-cost averaging. But where is the logic behind taking more money from what is presumably a personal interest-bearing account, for the purpose of growing the size of a non-interest bearing account where most of the money is dormant on any given day, and where a starting sum that a person can afford to lose has already been established?

. . .

NATURALLY, A LAS Vegas resident has a big edge being able to wager with cash on the fly, at the best available line at easily accessible outlets. An online wagerer, by comparison, is forced to keep three accounts open in an attempt at securing the best possible line and could get painted into a corner if one account balance gets too low and, for instance, the four best lines happen to be offered by that particular sportsbook where the balance is lower than the sum of the intended wagers. Full-time professional point-spread investors work out of Las Vegas. For anyone else doing it anywhere else, easy-to-forget financial details are obstacles to maximizing long-term profit. For that reason, anyone outside of Las Vegas needs to keep their expectations low because nearly every supposedly "sharp" preparation they are advised to make—like using three online sports books—can be shot down in three seconds by anyone who has passed Finance 101. Shopping for the best available line has long been one of the golden rules of sports wagering. Nobody wants to lose by a half-point when they could have pushed. Nobody wants to push when they could have won. But the drawback to having multiple online accounts is being spread thin from the start by mere virtue of establishing them. Which is one reason why I always say, "Pick games that cover by 10 points!" It has been written that having multiple sources will "never" hurt the player. The writers of that rule should try telling that to online players whose books have vaporized. Would the player rather lose one or two same-size wagers a season by a half-point, or see two-thirds of the intended seasonal investment pull a disappearing act when the online sports book suddenly goes out of business?

Speaking of 10 points, that is the average margin vs. the point-spread per game in the NFL. Which means that half-point "insurance" offered by sports books is a bad buy. A sportsbook offering +3 will give the bettor +3.5 for 12/10, and the bettor who takes it is unaware that the half-point will come into play in only about one out of every eight NFL games. Will the half-point sucker be on that game? If so, will the half-point sucker be on the right side? The half-point sucker easily forgets that his side might lose by 4 points, or 6 points, or 8 points, and that he has a better chance of losing at 12/10 for no reason, than of winning at 12/10 when he could have won at the standard 11/10.

Speaking of 10 points again, that represents the extra margin per side or total in a three-team teaser bet. Instead of Atlanta +3, Arizona +7, and Baltimore –3, a three-team teaser grants the player Atlanta +13, Arizona +17, Baltimore +7. All three must cover, ties lose. Remember, the average margin vs. the spread per game is 10 points. So where is the edge for the bettor in a 10-point tease that pays even money? There is none. Same goes for the other teaser offering: 6 points with two teams. When you have to win more than one side to cash a wager, and the average outcome can cause a loss, it's not a good bet.

Money-line wagering—no spread, just picking the winner with odds—rarely offers the true price. New York Giants bettors were ecstatic to win $350 for every $100 wagered on Big Blue against the New England Patriots in Super Bowl XLII. How many of them knew that the true payoff should have been about $515 for every $100? Meanwhile, losing with the Patriots at $400 to win $100 in that game was like losing four games at once. Pick your poison. Or, pass.

Parlays, teasers, propositions, and futures are like the house's table and wheel games in a casino. Anyone can play one, and win. But over time, the payoffs do not match the true odds. There is probably a sports book owner out there right now having a "How to Get Rich Quick by Betting Teasers, Propositions, and Parlays" book ghost-written for him. Good luck if you buy the hype. You'll need it.

20

College Football and the Future

C OLLEGE FOOTBALL VS. the point-spread is a book in itself. Similarities and differences from the NFL exist. One of the differences is that unlike the NFL, certain bettors can speak with their wallets and attempt to influence margins in certain situations. It does not mean that the bettors actually possess the power to do it. But in their lead-in to the 2007 season, *The Columbian*, serving Clark County in the state of Washington, put forth this particular scenario:

> *Betting on college and professional sports is a multibillion dollar business. Every Saturday afternoon, there are some sitting in the stands of a game in Martin Stadium or Husky Stadium more concerned about the point spread than who's ahead. Washington State Athletic Director Jim Sterk recalls a game in 2002 when then-WSU coach Mike Price had his quarterback take a knee to run out the clock near the goal line rather than try to score—and cover the point spread—in preserving a win over Arizona. Later that night, Sterk received a phone call from an angry booster who lost thousands because the Cougars didn't cover the spread, and therefore said to forget about his annual donation.*

Money talks! Or, at the very least, attempts to speak and demands to be heard. They will not discuss it publicly, they will not risk losing a game or angering the future opponent for the sake of covering a point-spread, and evidence of "pouring it on" for the sake of loyal rooters who might have a vested interest in their favorite team is mostly circumstantial. But where there is smoke from burnt losing tickets, there are fired coaches. I've always thought that one of the reasons why the University of Florida "rooting" community had such a quick hook with Ron Zook was the contrast in ATS records between Zook and Steve Spurrier, the head coach he replaced in 2002 before being fired after 2004. Whether both coaches were going all-out all the time and not saving anything for later is open for debate, but there is no denying the record. In Spurrier's last two seasons as Florida head coach, the Gators were 17-6 ATS as the favorite, consistently clearing a monstrous average of three and four scores per game. Spurrier, the UF coach for 12 seasons, had a well-earned reputation for being a bully. But in Zook's first two seasons, the Gators were 3-13 ATS in games they were "supposed to win," despite an average lay that was down to two and three scores per favored outing.

When certain people have developed an entitlement to 74 percent successes, and are suddenly taken down to 81 percent failures in the same situation, you can bet they'll be attempting to voice their influence. Gator Nation wasn't all that pleased with Zook's successor Urban Meyer when he delivered them a pair of 4-6 ATS seasons in 2005 and 2006. It just so happened that after a series of "underwhelming" performances in Meyer's second season, Florida rooters and financial backers nevertheless woke up and discovered their team in the BCS Championship Game at the end of 2006. As the +8 underdog, the Gators humiliated Ohio State to claim the National Championship. Suddenly, Meyer was forever their genius.

The median team rate of favorite coverage in college football is 49 percent. From 2002 to 2006, there was only one team and coach that came close to matching Spurrier's top-level success rate as a habitual favorite: Bobby Petrino. During his five seasons at Louisville, Petrino's teams, already with a multi-score lead, would drive the field in hurry-up mode and eventually clear rather large point-spreads in the fourth quarter en route to running up a 30-15 ATS record (67 percent) as the favorite. After Petrino left Louisville for the NFL following the 2006 season, elite coverage rate by Louisville as a favorite was followed by a 1-6-1 ATS season when favored under first-season head coach Steve Kragthorpe. Talk about your angry mobs! Only four games into Kragthorpe's tenure, www.firekragthorpenow.com was established. The site's mission, of course, was "dedicated to the removal of Steve Kragthorpe as head coach of the University of Louisville." On it, the ex-coach was referred to as "Saint Petrino."

Kragthorpe, Zook and all collegiate head coaches exist in a different environment than the NFL. From a marketing perspective, teams within college football conferences combine to operate as individual cooperatives. The National Collegiate Athletic Association (NCAA) is merely the organizing and governing body for the sports within it. The NCAA once negotiated television contracts for all of college football. Had those contracts still been in effect with ESPN, CBS, and ABC in 1984, they would have distributed $74 million to about 100 member schools. Which, in 1981, had prompted member schools Oklahoma and Georgia to file a suit against the NCAA's television plan, stating that it constituted many inappropriate business factors illegal under the Sherman Act. The court ruled in favor of the schools, citing anti-trust violations. Within 12 years, the deal between Georgia's Southeastern Conference and CBS was worth about $20 million to the 12 schools within it. Within another 12 years, conference broadcast rights were approaching $30 to $40 million per conference, which had created their own personal money pies—with bigger slices for everyone. Conferences that split into divisions so that Conference Championship Games could be played—and therefore televised and sold—created even bigger pies.

The goal of any reasonably good college football team is to win its conference and play in the best (most financially lucrative) bowl for which they are eligible when the season begins. As games are played and wins and losses are established, the conference standings and bowl pecking order sorts itself out. As of 2007, the meaningful college football universe (where teams represented wagering interests) consisted of 119 teams within 11 conferences, plus independents Notre Dame, Army, and Navy. Conferences have multiple tie-ins to bowls. For instance, the team with sixth-best record in the Pac-10 plays in the Insight Bowl on New Year's Eve and the team with the third-best record in the Big Ten Conference plays in the Outback Bowl on New Year's Day. Champions of the Atlantic Coast Conference (ACC), Big East, Big Ten, Big 12, Pac 10 and SEC play in the most lucrative, $10–$15 million Bowl Championship Series games (BCS), and if any of them happen to be ranked first or second in the nation, they face each other in the BCS Championship Game to determine the national champion.

Within that Straight-Up college football environment, many of the same ATS World practical preparations and tactical applications covered in this "NFL" book will also apply. For instance, our 2007 *Zone Blitz* noted that Michigan was the "luckiest team in America" during the 2006 season, recovering fumbles at the nation's highest rate, and losing the fewest number of their own fumbles (4). When Michigan lost in "historic" fashion to Division 1-AA Appalachian State in the 2007 opener (the Wolverines would have been a –39 favorite had a point-spread been offered), the result shocked all sports followers in the nation except for me. How could I have been shocked after labeling Michigan as the single luckiest team of the prior season? You *expect* last season's luckiest team to lose in grand fashion, ASAP!

Northern Illinois was a 4-8 ATS team with a +2 TO Ratio in 2006. They proceeded to graduate the entire starting offensive line and a four-year starter at running back. The offensive coordinator was hired away by Georgia Tech. They had tied Michigan for the fewest amount of fumbles lost in 2006. When a team is +2 in Turnover Ratio but only 33 percent ATS, as Northern Illinois had been, the last thing it needs is to lose experienced veterans with sloppier play almost guaranteed to be on the way. By season's end, what do you know? Instead of only 4 lost fumbles, the cough-it-up frequency rose by more than 300 percent to –13. With 19 interceptions tossing gasoline on the fire, the team went from a TO Ratio of +2 in 2006, to –17. Only a 10-point deflation in their average line allowed Northern Illinois to eventually be 4-6-1 ATS in 2007. But from

Opening Day through the month of October, Northern Illinois covered only one game against the spread! Anyone who did their off-season due diligence and uncovered this team's depleted resources and weak positioning created an opportunity to be 6-1 by "going against" Northern Illinois from the start. When you win six out of seven games against one team, you are in position to opt out while way ahead, ready to attack other opportunities just as fools rush into the party late to be 0-3 ATS going against the same team. When the opportunity exists to win six out of seven games against one team, you can actually tailor a lean, mean season plan to do nothing but go against that team from the start. Hey, why not? Who's stopping you?

But always keep tuned to the big picture because what appears to be a slam-dunk could get sideswiped. Teams in characteristically regressive beginning situations have a greater chance to encounter teams with more issues than they have. Teams in characteristically strong "move-up" situations have a greater chance to encounter teams with strengths in other areas that trump their own strengths. Also, with four times as many teams and rosters 60 percent larger than the NFL, new impact players and injuries can mess up the best-laid early assessments and force you to move away from pre-season plans to attack "on" or "against" certain teams.

Because there are four times more college football teams than NFL franchises, the talent gap between best and worst team is wider. Statistics tend to run accordingly, with a greater gap between high and low medians and averages in both Straight-Up and ATS categories. For instance, in the NFL, the high-low ATS Margins in a given season tend to run from +7.0 at the top, to −7.0 at the bottom. In college football, the gap is wider with an ATS Margin high-low range that tends to span from about +12.0 down to −12.0.

In the eight seasons from 2000 to 2007, only eight NFL teams scored more than 30 points per game over the course of the regular season and only one team allowed more than 30 points per game in that span. At the same time, things were much different in college football. In 2007 alone, six college teams scored 40 or more points per game, another 40 teams scored from 30.0 to 38.9 points per game. On the other side of the scoreboard that season, three college teams allowed more than 40 points per game and another 41 allowed from 30.3 to 39.7. Defense is at a premium in the college ranks, a prime reason being that many coaches attempt to convert their best defensive athletes—especially the ones with the most speed—to offense. These new running backs and wide receivers thin the talent pool on defensive depth charts. Defensive lines also tend to get stocked with linemen who are converted offensive tight ends. As they lose speed, teams gain inexperience. To help get a handle on what is normal in college football, overall statistics and facilitate separating fact from reporting hype, you can compare NFL and college offensive medians in Figure 20-2.

Coordinator analysis, and Year One and Year Two coaching regime inspections will yield similar trends as in the NFL. Be on the lookout for a poor Year One when it follows a good final year by the departed coaching regime. That's what the beleaguered Ron Zook and Steve Kragthorpe walked into at Florida and Louisville. The trend was in evidence in 2007, when five of the twenty-three Year One coaching staffs joined teams that had profitable records against the spread the year before. Of their five teams, four regressed into net loss range vs. the spread. The four included Central Michigan, even though Central Michigan covered more games than anyone else in the nation in 2006, and even though CMU was on its way to winning the MAC Championship for the second consecutive season in 2007!

Then there is better-than-average Year One to lower-than-average Year Two. In 2006, Bret Bielema of Wisconsin was the only Year One coach among nine whose team covered at least 60 percent ATS. In his Year Two, Wisconsin posted the worst point-spread record—4-8 ATS—among those nine teams.

For bad Year One to good Year Two, George O'Leary's 2005 Central Florida team was the ultimate model. O'Leary spent 2004 moving defensive players to offense and offensive players to defense. His assistants taught and the players carried out the lessons over the course of a brutal schedule not made by O'Leary's hand. Almost every game was actually a scrimmage for Central Florida, which finished 0-11 SU, 3-8 ATS. Who would expect a competitive, profitable team in 2006? Me! What did not kill them would make them stronger, but at the same time undervalued. What was 3-8 ATS suddenly became 8-4 ATS, including a 6-1 ATS run as soon as the Conference USA season started. September's non-conference games are often as the treated as exhibitions by many college coaches

NFL	Hi	Lo	CF	Hi	Lo
2007	6.6	−5.8	2007	11.8	−11.0
2006	6.9	−4.7	2006	10.9	−9.1
2005	6.2	−5.8	2005	11.7	−9.4
2004	8.9	−6.2	2004	13.8	−8.6
2003	5.6	−8.3	2003	14.0	−12.5
2002	5.9	−5.9	2002	14.4	−15.0
2001	8.5	−6.3	2001	9.8	−13.7
2000	7.3	−8.6	2000	12.9	−12.8

FIGURE 20-1 Team ATS margins, NFL vs. College

not in the running for the national championship. Being poised to be "on" the winless team from the prior the season when the real bell rang for the next created another happy "opt-out ahead" situation for later.

• • •

As MENTIONED EARLIER in this chapter, covering the entirety of college football vs. the point-spread could be a whole new book. So let's take one game that comprises many fascinating facets of this art, exercise, practice, whatever you want to call it, as a model for instruction: the 2007 Armed Forces Bowl between California (–4.5) and Air Force.

Air Force's offense had gained 419 yards per game in the regular season, California's 395. By virtue of more teams in the college game, there are more offensive styles featured and this particular style matchup was about as contrasting as it gets. California utilized a pro-style offense. Many players choose to play at Cal as a stepping-stone to the NFL and at the time, ex-Cal football players on NFL rosters outnumbered ex-Air Force players 30 to 1. Their average play selection was 32 running plays, 35 passes per game-in the top 30 of pass-skewed offenses in the nation. Meanwhile, the Air Force offensive system called for them to run the ball more frequently (77 percent of offensive plays) and throw it fewer times than any other team in the nation except for Navy. At first thought, Air Force's style might have seemed too predictable to succeed against any competent opponent, especially a Pac-10 passing team with future NFL players on both sides of the line of scrimmage. "Conventional wisdom"—the kind you almost always want to avoid—would usually knee-jerk this kind of situation as a no-brainer for the small favorite if the small favorite owned Cal's assets, assuming it could easily exploit Air Force's assets.

But with different formations, fakes, and options on every running play, it is common knowledge among both Straight-Up and ATS Men that preparing to face the Air Force offense is usually a nightmare for opposing defensive coordinators, and an ultimate challenge for that coordinator's players. More than one week between games is generally considered to be necessary to help defend against a rare, unfamiliar system and although Cal would have that, they still fell

MEDIANS	RA	RY	RYPC	PC	PA	PY	Comp%	YPA	YPG
NFL	27	111	3.9	19	32	217	60.2%	6.7	322
COLLEGE	38	144	3.7	18	31	222	58.4%	7.1	372

FIGURE 20-2 Team ATS margins, NFL vs. College

behind 21-0 in the first quarter as their defensive players were repeatedly aban-
doning their responsibility, resulting in long Air Force runs after Cal players were
faked out of their jockstraps. Meanwhile, Air Force's first-string defense did not
have a freshman or sophomore on it. In terms of experience, that unit—though
overmatched physically—might have owned the most veteran—not to mention
most disciplined—defense in the nation.

The flip side of the matchup was that California enjoyed a size disparity on
its offensive line vs. Air Force's smaller defense, and was also stocked with some
of the fastest and potentially most productive wide receivers in the nation.
A 21-0 deficit for a run-based team like Air Force would have been death. A 21-
0 deficit for a team whose most dynamic players are wide receivers is an excit-
ing hurdle to clear, especially when it has a quarterback who can get the ball
to them against a smaller, slower defense. When Cal's head coach Jeff Tedford
yanked his habitually underachieving senior starting quarterback and replaced
him early in the second quarter with an unfamiliar backup with a stronger arm
and better mobility, the game was just beginning. Air Force's defense had no
book on the backup, and Cal's defense was getting wiser to Air Force's offense
as the game progressed. The gap narrowed: 21-7, and then 21-14 at halftime.
The third quarter began with Air Force moving down the field but stalling late,
settling for a field goal. From that point on, Cal would score four touchdowns,
and Air Force three field goals. Bad trade-off for Air Force, especially after
their starting quarterback got knocked out of the game when tackled on Cal's
1-yard-line on a sneak, further diminishing the Air Force offensive productiv-
ity. California led 42-30 with 3:24 remaining and was already up to 470 yards
of offense, preparing to power the ball to the finish against the exhausted Air
Force defense. But the Falcons caught a break when Cal fumbled on the first
play from scrimmage at their own 34-yard-line. Air Force's offense took the
ball on the short field and scored a touchdown within six plays. With 2:33
remaining in the fourth quarter, the pre-extra point score was 42-36. At that
point, any bettor involved in the game with either side has gotten involved
in something that was destined to be a sweat job—a game where each team
was able to exploit the other almost equally, as far as the point-spread was
concerned. Cal, the −4.5 favorite, led by 6 points. Nobody with either Cal −4.5
or Air Force +4.5 was a genius, but it looked like Cal backers were going to win
the bet anyway, barring an Air Force miracle.

Wait a minute! It's doubtful that any coach's handbook says to go for the two-
point conversion when trailing by 6 points. But that's what Air Force head coach
Troy Calhoun chose to do, attempting to cut the deficit to 4, which would have
been a half-point within the spread. Was the spread the reason? Nobody knows,
nobody asked. You could reason that by cutting the lead to 4, then getting the
onsides kick recovery and a late, go-ahead touchdown to lead by 3 instead of

2 would create a situation where a Cal field goal at the end of regulation could only tie the game for overtime, not win it in regulation. These military guys are always a few steps ahead of the opponent, but was Calhoun really thinking that far ahead?

Hope was floated, but quickly sank. Air Force's two-point conversion failed, as did the onsides kick recovery. But Troy Calhoun won the respect of a lot of people that afternoon, including *Sports Reporter* followers who went with a published pick on Air Force +4.5. In their eyes, the coach was a hero.

One factor omitted at the start of this particular example demonstrates the exclusive neighborhood where the smartest of ATS World residents live. Two of California's crack group of wide receivers had been suspended for the first quarter of the bowl game for breaking team rules. When the coach replaced the starting quarterback trailing 21-0, he also brought the suspendees into the lineup for the first time that afternoon. "They were chomping at the bit to get in," coach Tedford told wire services. "They were prancing around on the sideline. And so when they finally got let loose, they were ready to roll."

"It gave them a spark," Air Force linebacker Drew Fowler said. "As soon as they got in, it was a different story." Playing only the last three quarters, DeShawn Jackson and Robert Jordan still accounted for 11 receptions and 229 of Cal's 305 receiving yards.

· · ·

SOME READERS MAY know this already, some may not: bookmakers offer halftime point-spreads on almost all NFL and college football games. The smartest football bettors in America that afternoon were the ones who put four things together, two at a time, regarding the Armed Forces Bowl:

1) Air Force's confusing offense could do business early.
2) Air Force's defense would catch a break in the first half, given the announced absence of two Cal wide receivers. Conclusion—first half: Air Force, +2/21–14 winner.
3) These Cal wide receivers are making a one-sided joke of this game.
4) Air Force's defense cannot make a stop now that Cal has regained the balance in their offensive attack, and as the game wears on, it will only get worse for them. Conclusion—second half: Cal, –3/28-15 winner.

Is this splitting of a game into two parts cutting it too fine? Did they tell Enrico Fermi that he was cutting it too fine after he split the atom? No. They gave him a Nobel Prize!

Winning a pair of "half" bets on each of the opposing sides in the same game, by 9 and 10 points apiece, is not cutting it too fine. It represents the fine-tuned, real time cutting edge at its best. At the same time, a full game player at the spread of 4.5 was enduring a see-saw, possibly stressful zig-zagging affair with bizarre elements in play, whose outcome vs. the spread was in doubt almost to the end no matter which side was staked. Sometime in the future, the "regular" football bettor will be thinking and acting in the manner of the mysterious minority winning both halves of the same game with two different sides. Football forecasters with razor-sharp instincts making behind-the-scenes, real-time, atom-splitting progress in the present are raising the bar for everyone who will be involved down the road.

Acknowledgments

THIS BOOK IS written with reverence to Andy Beyer, whose 1975 work *Picking Winners*, and subsequent books on horse racing have been an inspiration for their passionate instruction on how to refine one's approach to become more successful in a popular "niche" activity. Beyer, the *Washington Post* horse racing writer, always claimed to be a handicapper who writes, not a writer who handicaps. But as a near-Harvard grad writing for a mixed audience, he always got his message across loud and clear. His landmark achievements in Thoroughbred racing analysis raised the bar for the few who have since dared to try to build upon related "alternative forecasting" methods that Beyer brought into the mainstream.

A debt of gratitude goes to the *Daily Racing Form*, whose ever-changing powers-that-be had the serendipitous sense to turn one of its best writers into what they call a handicapper. Without the learned foundation of between-the-lines interpretation of horse racing past performances, there is no *How to Beat the Pro Football Pointspread*.

Sincere homage and respect are overdue for input received, past and present, from: Jerry Keller, a New York business publisher, for hammering home the point that the goal of any publication should be to help make the reader more successful; Greg Gallo, sports editor of the *New York Post*, for demonstrating how to do things a certain way without compromising; Lindsay Hamilton, for faith, broad-minded guidance and constructive criticism; Dad and Joe, for long-term lessons in the value and benefits of working hard and investing wisely; Smokin' Willy, for playing the role of Great Gazoo; all readers of *Sports Reporter*, for their loyalty, trust and willingness to explore different realms; and author and documentary film writer Sam Toperoff, for lunch and a simple piece of sound advice about how to create a spark.

About the Author

BOBBY SMITH IS the Editor of *Sports Reporter* and sportsreporter.com, where he writes and directs projection reports on NFL and college football, NBA and college basketball, and thoroughbred horserace wagering. He is the author of *Sports Reporter Zone Blitz*, an annual almanac that forecasts all NFL and College Football teams' investment prospects vs. the point-spread for the upcoming season, using proprietary formulas developed and refined to help correctly target generally unforeseen changes in team investment value and performance. He is also the former Editor of *American Turf Monthly* magazine—the nation's oldest horse racing monthly—and a former columnist and analyst for the *Daily Racing Form* in California and New Jersey. A graduate of St. John's University in New York, he and his wife live in Long Island, New York, and look forward to becoming adoptive parents.